Being MADE for Ministry

Tony Shomari Marshall

To the memory of my father

Deacon Tony "Pop" Marshall,

The love of my wife Chantell, my mother Judy,

and my daughters Tiajah and Talaya

Tony Shomari Marshall

CONTENTS

Tony Shomari Marshall

ACKNOWLEDGMENTS

This work would not have been possible without the life and ministry of several people. I acknowledge the legacies of Bishops William Rimson, Walter Bogan and Clifford Dunlap for providing excellent examples of Godly leadership. To Bishop Rance Allen who has become a father figure to me I am much appreciative. To my colleagues in chaplaincy and supervision that continue to sharpen my skills I am grateful. To the many students I have worked with over the years I am yet humble to have served you, and I enjoy watching you grow into your God given purpose. I am thankful for the ministry of Janice Tucker my photographer at Luvable Media. A special word of appreciation to my editor, Timeka Tounsel, Ph.D. words cannot express your value in getting this project from my thoughts to print, you are so very encouraging and gifted. To the members of the House of Prayer Institutional Church Family for letting me share a bit of myself with you. Finally without the sacrifice of my wife, Chantell, and the love of my daughters Tiajah Shomara and Talaya Shomar this project, much like everything else in my life would be void of meaning. I love and thank you all so much.

Blessed Journey

1   THE DIVINE PLAN

FOR WE ARE GOD'S CREATION, BEING MADE THROUGH
CHRIST TO DO MINISTRY, MINISTRY THAT GOD HAS
ALREADY PLANNED THAT WE SHOULD LIVE OUT IN
OUR LIVES
EPHESIANS 2.10

I once had the pleasure of stumbling upon a street artist as she created beauty right before my eyes. I watched as she arranged colors and unidentified shapes into symmetry and objects. I marveled with bewilderment as she turned shades and textures into perception and reality. I was at a loss of breath at the exact moment when this mass confusion of colors and shapes transformed from her feeble hands into an image of beauty for me, its beholder. On that day I learned not to judge a work of art while it is still under construction. What initially may appear to be chaos and confusion actually reflects order and structure that will blossom into beauty at the appropriate time.

I have grown to understand how God interacts with me in much the same way that the artist worked on that painting in the park. Often times what I perceive to be painful and disordered is really a masterpiece in process. I now believe that my seemingly chaotic and hectic life is becoming a pure gift of God to the body of

Christ. Perhaps I have value and purpose the likes of which I never imagined and maybe this is truth for you as well.

While beauty can be found in all sorts of places like the arts, literature, and architecture, it is most vivid in the tapestry of human life. We all enjoy watching people harness their God given artistic nature to bring beauty and value to our world, but how much more glory does God receive when that same power is demonstrated through the lives that the people of God live? This is the essence of life and ministry, the art of living a Christian life to its fullest. The beauty of God is revealed in us when we yield our entire being to God's creative power, not just in one single moment of life, but in the constellation of moments woven together in a life well lived. This is the kind of life that brings our Heavenly Father great joy.

Friend, God has a plan for our lives that will reveal the Glory and beauty of God if we choose to follow it. The only way to access that beauty is to identify your unique ministry and then live it out in your daily life. Paul expressed this very thought in Ephesians 2.10, *For we are God's creation, being made through Christ to do ministry, ministry that God has already planned that we should live out in our lives.*

Once I fully understood this teaching, I began to observe and reflect upon how God was moving and working through, in and with my life. My ministry is at the heart of my relationship with God and is the entire purpose for my being and existence. I believe that we are all called to a life that is so in harmony with God's plan that our entire beings become beautiful mosaics of ministry that honor the King.

So you see, there is no aspect of life that is void of God's influence and purpose. The clothes I wear, the things I eat, my sources of entertainment are all divinely influenced for life and ministry. As believers we are designed for ministry, and yet, many believers still struggle with the concept that God utilizes our whole person for ministry.

In my 25 years of ministry one of the most frequently asked questions I have received from those searching is: what is the will of God for my life? One day a young man named Henry contacted me and arranged to meet me in my office. He informed me that God called him to the ministry. As I explored this notion further with him he explained that he actually had no idea what God desired of him, and that he wanted to be cautious about accepting such a tremendous task.

Importantly, Henry expressed that he was open to whatever God desired. After all, he was no stranger to service. Henry had spent years serving young people in different non-profit organizations at camps and retreat centers. He donated his time and finances to support those endeavors and was personally involved in several mentoring relationships with other young men. The painful childhood that he suffered motivated Henry to serve young men in similar situations. Henry didn't serve in spite of his pain, he served because of it. His aim was to be a positive role model like the one he received in his late teen years from an aging clergyman.

AFTER HENRY POURED OUT HIS SOUL TO ME I

RESPONDED, "HENRY, YOU'VE BEEN IN MINISTRY YOUR WHOLE LIFE." There was such a beauty in Henry's retelling of his life story. I could hear, feel and sense the love that he shares with those troubled and adjudicated young men.

I was most moved by the fact that despite his great efforts, Henry never considered himself special, just a Christian and a faithful servant. He desired no elevated seat or haughty title, he just wanted to help others the same way Christ had led someone else to help him. In his humility Henry failed to see that he was already busy doing the work of the Lord. Really every day that he spent mentoring and guiding those young men the world had written off Henry was living out the call of ministry on his life.

The Apostle Peter teaches us, in 1 Peter 2.5,9 that all believers *are being built into a holy and royal priesthood.* Thus, I wanted Henry to understand that he, and all those called of God, are called to live a life of service. That is to say that we are all ministers of the Gospel. Yes, you, my sisters and brothers, are indeed ministers of the Gospel of Christ.

God's ministry is much larger than the pulpit inside of the church building. God is and is active everywhere. Over time this fundamental teaching of the Protestant church has faded and been replaced by a hierarchical, non-Biblical understanding of ministry.[i] The church has been tricked into thinking that only certain people with special titles, positions and I dare say, anointing, are called to be servants and ministers. This is the exact opposite of the Biblical truth. Peter declares that we are all priests. The New Testament church was built upon the idea that everyone had a part to play in the kingdom of God. Consequently, ministry is not restricted to vocation, it is a lifestyle that we all are called to live.

God's Plan is to Make Us

In returning to the central text in Ephesians 2.10 there are several notable things to observe. First, Paul teaches that, "We are God's creation." Once we have accepted the gift of salvation through faith in Jesus Christ we are a new creation of God. Old things are passed away and all things are new. When "newness" is applied to our service it is not all instantaneously complete, rather we are continually becoming new. Every day we are being made into what God desires; we are always under construction.

The tension presented in the Scripture is that of being a new creation and yet being made new. The work of that new creation is not instantaneously complete; rather God is continually working on us throughout our lives. God uses our life experiences and our relationships (with God, self, and others) to make us into the masterpieces He wants us to become. It is through these aspects of our Spirit or personhood that we are being formed—we are all works in progress.

I must warn you that the transformative process of becoming a new creation in Christ is no easy journey. The pain, shame, and struggles that we experience are all a part of the process of being made. When we embrace these trying times as teachable moments, we make room for God to do good work in and through us.

So, my brothers and sisters, how is God yet making you into who you are? Can you see the hand of God pushing and pulling you to be better than you are? God is molding you into a new creation so that you can serve others to God's glory.

I truly believe that all truth is God's truth. Thus, I find it so interesting that much leading thought today in the areas of psychology and behavioral sciences reflect the teachings of the Scriptures. Such is the case with the concept that God is continually making us. The concept here is simple; God is making you into who you are to become on a daily basis. When I hear this I think of modern developmental thought, which suggests that an individual's entire life of events, relationships, preparation, pitfalls and triumphs all culminate in the masterpiece of who they become. [ii]

It is commonly believed that people develop continually throughout life. For example, within developmental thought our personalities are constantly changing. Through different crisis events in life we mature and are molded into who we are to be. Hence, to borrow a term from Erik Erikson, our learning is epigenetic in nature.[iii] Our learned behavior builds upon past experiences and is integrated thoroughly through all as aspects of our being.

Similarly, God uses our past experiences and learning, through the aid of the Holy Spirit, to prepare us to be who we need to be today and tomorrow. All of our experiences of life play a role in shaping us into who we become emotionally, spiritually and intellectually.[iv] So, how is God using your past learned behaviors and attitudes to bring about glory in your current situations? Here are some of the key lessons that you can learn through the events of your life, or as I call it, the classroom of life.

The Classroom of Life

The classroom of life is made up of all your relationships and experiences, and allows for learning to occur whenever and wherever you are open to receive it. This classroom includes the good and bad things that come your way that are seemingly beyond your control. Yet, the things that happen and the people whom you encounter do not emerge by chance, but by divine planning.

Oftentimes people miss the lessons that God has for them because they do not like the form or package in which the lesson comes to them. Brothers and sisters, even if we do not like the teacher or the classroom, we are still responsible for learning the lesson. In other words, you might not like the person that God has chosen to connect you to for any particular lesson, but you still must learn the lesson. With this mindset we can embrace the fact that nothing is accidental and can find the benefit in all things, just as Paul explained in Romans 8.28: *And we know that in all things God works for the good of those that are loving God, and who have been called according to his purpose.*

As I reflect on the power of finding lessons in unlikely sources, I'm reminded of an experience I had in college. It was the dead of winter during my junior year and I had driven through a storm to hear a preacher that had come to town. It was one of those negative temperature days of blowing snow and icy roads. Many cars were

9

stranded as I traveled and I contemplated turning around. I was persistent because I needed to hear an on time word from the Lord. The joyful expectation that had kept me from turning around in the middle of that storm was completely lost by the time the preacher reached the middle of his sermon. His message was loosely strung together with no cohesive thought or transitional flow. He relied upon charm and rhythmic cadence of voice, rather than content, to move the crowd.

Upon returning to campus the next day I was asked what I thought of the message from the previous evening. I expressed that I learned nothing at all about the delivery of the Gospel message. My professor, Dr. Ronald S. Collymore, corrected me and stated that I learned a great lesson, for I had learned what *not* to do. It wasn't the lesson that I was expecting, but it was a valuable lesson nonetheless. Professor Collymore's statement reminded me that once we get past our frustrations and disappointments, we can see the lesson in nearly any experience. If we prayerfully talk to God about the things happening around us, we will see that there is always a lesson to be learned.

One of the areas of life where we can learn the most is in the people whom God chooses to place around us, specifically, our families. God has chosen the time and circumstances of your birth, life and death. It was prearranged to whom you would be born and where you would develop. If the totality of your life is the product of God's deliberate design, then you can be certain that there is some measure of growth, learning and development that can be derived from all aspects of your story.

For instance, did you know that your family of origin is a significant learning environment for your growth and maturity? No, you may not have been able to choose the family that you were born into, but your place of origin was strategically set in place by God for His Glory and your purpose. God has designed our development such that there are lessons that you and I need and can only get from our environment and family of origin. These lessons will be useful in fulfilling what God has planned for us.

Once we accept that God is the master designer in control of what happens in our lives, we have to stop fighting God's plan. Yes, God's plan will be difficult, scary and even painful at times. Nevertheless, the proper response for us as believers is to stop fighting life and live it. Make the decision to learn from your environment no matter what. Choose to glean lessons from your family of origin regardless of how difficult that task seems.

If we return to Henry's story we see a clear example of what it looks like when an individual decides to surrender to God's plan, even when that means enduring struggles. As Henry aged, he looked back over his life and realized that the longing he had as a young boy is the exact thing that God used to fuel is ministry. Henry became for other young men the type of mentor that was missing from his own life for must of his childhood. God used the painful experience of growing up without a positive male role model to shape Henry into a man that lived out the principles of being a positive role model. He became what he never had for the Glory of God.

What really is Ministry?

In order to adopt this new way of thinking about how God uses people and experiences to prepare us for our purpose, we must develop an appropriate definition of ministry. I argue that ministry is not a vocation but a lifestyle. A life dedicated to serving God and the people of God through every aspect of our existence. This lifestyle is open to the free flowing activity of God's Holy Spirit whenever and wherever. To live like this we must learn to look for God's activity all around us.

I have come to understand that there are some people in religious leadership who view ministry simply as a vocation. I have friends ordained as ministers in most of the mainline Christian denominations. Due to my work as a certified chaplain and supervisor, I also have very close friends and students that are leaders in non-Christian faith traditions. To some of them ministers are simply people that serve others for compensation. Those who walk in this belief set boundaries around ministry in much the same way that they would set boundaries around any other profession, that is to say that when a minister is not "at work" they are off duty and exempt from ministerial responsibilities. Ministers who serve in this way can easily separate when they are serving as a minister and when they are "off."

Since I embrace ministry as more than a 9-to-5, since I embrace it as a lifestyle, I cannot choose when God decides to work through me. To state it another way, I am never "off" or "on" because ministry is my life. It is who I am. Such a view of ministry is demonstrated most clearly in the life and ministry of Jesus.

When I look at the life of Jesus, I see him using all of himself and his surroundings to teach and serve others. He used his entire person to serve and minister. This is not to say that Christ never had a down moment; the Holy Scriptures record such moments like Mark 6.30-32:

> The apostles returned to Jesus and told him all that they had done and taught. And he said to them, "Come away by yourselves to a desolate place and rest a while."

Another such recording is John 4.6: *Since Jesus was tired from his journey, he sat by the well.*

Certainly, Jesus took part in human activities such as rest, meal times and festivals, but he also used whatever was happening in these seemingly mundane tasks to create teachable moments. For in Matthew 12 it is recorded that because Jesus was hungry he decided to pick grain and eat and use this as a teachable moment in life.

> At that time Jesus went through the grain fields on the Sabbath. He and his disciples were hungry and began to pick some grain to eat. When the Pharisees saw this, they said to him, "Look! Your disciples are doing what is unlawful on the Sabbath."
>
> He answered, "Haven't you read what David did when he and his companions were hungry? He entered the house of God, and he and his

*companions ate the consecrated bread, which was not lawful for them to do,
but only for the priest. Or haven't you read in the Law that the priests on
the Sabbath duty in the temple desecrate the Sabbath and yet are innocent? I
tell you that something greater than the temple is here. If you had known
what these words mean, 'I desire mercy, not sacrifice,' you would not have
condemned the innocent. For the Son of Man is Lord of the Sabbath."*

Jesus used their hunger as a moment to teach his true identity as the
Lord over the Sabbath. This wonderful teachable moment only
occurred because they were physically hungry.

Another such example occurs in Matthew 21. After arriving at
Jerusalem, Jesus decides to spend the night at Bethany. It is recorded
in chapter 21, verse 18.

*Early in the morning, as Jesus was on his way back to the city, he was
hungry. Seeing a fig tree by the road, he went up to it but found nothing on it
except leaves. Then he said to it, "May you never bear fruit again!"
Immediately the tree withered. When the disciples saw this, they were
amazed. "How did the fig tree wither so quickly?" they asked. Jesus replied,
"Truly I tell you, if you have faith and do not doubt, not only can you do
what was done to the fig tree, but also you can say to this mountain, 'Go,
throw yourself into the sea,' and it will be done. If you believe, you will
receive whatever you ask for in prayer."*

Here Jesus used his hunger and a barren fig tree to teach the disciples
about faith. Once again these examples demonstrate that Jesus used
the circumstances of life to teach great truths.

Just as Jesus used events in the lives of the disciples as teachable
moments, God also utilizes the events of our lives as teachable

moments. Your moments of insufficiency, fear, doubt, and fatigue are all moments to learn lessons of faith, courage and determination. These moments mold us as God works on us and makes us fit for our purpose.

I can clearly see that the things happening in my life are happening so that God can teach me and those within my realm of influence. The same is true for you. There have been unpleasant events in your life that only occur so that you can experience the teachable moment. I now look back over my life and wonder how many times I missed the message because I was so concerned with physical issues such as hunger, lack or just annoyance. Have you missed powerful moments of truth in your life because you were staring at the barren tree instead of the Savior that was with you?

Returning to our thought in Ephesians, I believe that we are being molded into God's finished product so that we can live out our ministry. It is everyone's divine purpose: to be a minister unto the Gospel of Jesus Christ. Every believer should desire to become all that they are to become for the Gospel sake. Our purpose is to allow God to teach us through our struggles as we will walk right into our calling. The journey of life provides plenty of experiences, struggles and opportunities for you to develop. I propose that with proper reflections we can learn from our mistakes and develop the courage to be who we are called to be.

2 THE JOURNEY

THEN WAS JESUS LED UP OF THE SPIRIT INTO THE
WILDERNESS TO BE TEMPTED OF THE DEVIL
MATTHEW 4.1

One of the high points of my life was a trip I took to South
Africa with several ministers involved in the Sustaining Pastoral
Excellence program through the Ecumenical Theological Seminary.
This fellowship program allowed me to study and reflect upon my
own pastoral development while engaging with my peers. I recall
venturing out early one morning to experience the sights and sounds
of this distant and exciting land. We came upon Lion's Head
Mountain in Cape Town. Since we had been out very early in the
morning I chose to enjoy Lion's Head from the bus. I enjoyed what I
thought was a beautiful view from the bus but I was beckoned,
urged, and summoned to go up the path further on foot and see the
landscape up close.

Initially I did not feel any desire to go farther than where the bus
stopped. But I soon yielded to the persistent urge to see more and
began my journey. Although the journey was steep at times and
caused much effort on my part, the farther away I got from the bus,

the more I appreciated the beauty of this majestic mountain. There were many obstacles in my path that would work to deter me. The several hundred year old steps were broken and unstable. The grass was unkempt and presented an authentic but rugged appearance. About half way up I thought this might be as good of a view that I would experience today and maybe I should just turn back. With each step I felt the muscles in my legs chiming in that I should quit. Even the sun played its part in discouraging me from pursuing my goals but at a certain point I believe I became determined that this effort would not be for naught. Upon reaching the peak I saw the dramatic backdrop to the city of Cape Town and I thanked God for the push to take the journey. The clouds, sky, mountain range, and colors were all different from this higher point of view. Even my appreciation for the journey changed once I reached the pinnacle. What a difference the journey can make to our view and experience in life.

The journey I took on that hot morning in South Africa is a lot like the journey of preparation I have taken in ministry. For every rough moment of toil and sweat, there has been a equal or greater moment where I could step back and see the hand of God working things out in my favor.

Many people working in ministry want the anointing of God so that they can make an impact in the world. Yet, of those who long for God's blessing, few are willing to endure the journey that will prepare them to do God's work in excellence. Charisma, an expansive intellect and a magnetic personality are good traits, but these alone are not enough to sustain the calling and lifestyle of ministry. The journey of preparation, with all its highs and lows, is essential to any type of ministry. It is this collection of experiences that develops our relationship with God and allows Him to form us and make us. When you avoid the journey of preparation, you cheapen the gift that God has placed inside of you and stunt your own growth. Those that avoid the journey will never see things from God's perspective regarding their life and ministry.

Let's look at the ministry of Jesus as a model. The Gospel of Saint Matthew begins, as any good Jewish Gospel should, with a wonderful genealogy leading to the birth of a Savior. Matthew then explains the circumstances surrounding Christ's birth. From there he informs us of the mysterious figure known as John the Baptist and of the water baptism he preached. The story heightens with the baptism experience of Jesus, by John, in the river Jordan. Subsequently, God the Father speaks and publicly announces the arrival of His Son and His Son's ministry. This brings us to an encounter that will serve as our subject of study in this section, the temptation of Christ.

The Temptation of Christ: Matthew 4.1-11

Then Jesus was led by the Spirit into the wilderness to be tempted of the devil. And after he had fasted forty days and forty nights, he was hungry. And then the Tempter came to him and said, If you are the Son of God, speak to these stones that they might become loaves of bread. But he answered and said, It is written, Man shall not live by bread alone, but by every word that comes out of the mouth of God. Then the devil took him up to the holy city, and sat him on the highest peak of the temple, And said unto him, If you are the Son of God, throw yourself down: because it is written, He will give his angels orders concerning you: and in their hands they will hold you up, so that you won't hit your foot against a stone.

Jesus said unto him, It is written again, you shalt not tempt the Lord your God. Again, the devil took him up into an exceeding high mountain, and showed him all the kingdoms of the world, and their glory; And said unto him, All these things will I give to you, if thou will fall down and worship me. Then said Jesus unto him, you get away Satan: for it is written, You will worship the Lord your God, and him only shall you serve. Then the devil left him, and, the angels came and ministered unto him.

The Temptation Encounter

It should come as no surprise that deciding to dedicate your life to God and ministry is a serious matter. When considering such a lifestyle we should examine ourselves. Here is a sample of some of the questions one should ask:

- Has God looked into our world and selected me to accomplish a particular aspect of ministry?

- Is this really what God desires for me to do?

- Why am I pursuing public ministry?

- What do I expect to get from this?

- What am I willing to give up for the sake of ministry?

- Where is God leading me?

- How am I gifted for ministry?

- What type of ministry has God called me to?

As you can see, developing your ministry requires just as much thought as it does prayer and fasting. Internal motivations and desires should also be examined. Personal relationships should be re-evaluated. Certain aspects of your lifestyle may need to be altered.

This process of personal reflection is not a single occurrence, but rather an ongoing internal dialogue. As ministers, we much continually ask the question of why. Why should I pursue such a call and lifestyle? Importantly, in answering the question why we must identify our pure and impure motives. No one is immune to the appeal of status, material wealth, and power. Yet, when we become honest about our motives we can overcome these common temptations and seek a greater understand of ourselves as ministers.

The journey to a fulfilling and effective ministry begins right here, in the reflection stage. Only after we have devoted time to wrestling with these issues can we then proceed to travel down the road with God.

The people of God will see God's work, respect God's work and encourage God's work in you. This confirmation is a necessity. One cannot enter God's ministry and reflect God's Glory without public and private validation. While I understood that many contemporary ministers do not believe in a Divine call from God to a life of ministry, I still believe that this component of the journey is necessary. It is this very endorsement that sustains God's ministering servant during times of confrontation with the enemy. For even the Apostle Paul reflected upon his experience on the way to Damascus in the 22nd chapter of Acts when he gave his defense. That event became confirmation for Paul to endure the persecution and glorify God with his ministry and life. Thus I still believe that God is the agent that calls, validates, sends and accompanies the ministers into the world.

The Beginning of Jesus' Public Ministry

After you have become clear about the call of God on your life and begin to take the next steps in your ministry journey, you will experience highs and lows, trials and triumphs. Take heart, the things that you are experiencing are also things that Jesus Christ experienced at the beginning of His public ministry. Thus, we can use Jesus' ministry as a model and guide for our own.

And when Jesus was baptized, he immediately came up out of the water: and the heavens were opened, and he saw the Spirit of God descending like a dove, and lighting on him: And there was a voice coming out of the heavens saying, This is my beloved Son, I am well pleased. Then Jesus was led by the Spirit into the wilderness to be tempted of the devil. Matthew 3.16

Before Jesus began His earthly public ministry He had a moment of validation, which was His baptism. This incredible event displays several truths for us today. It is evident that before Jesus began a public ministry, He recognized the need for a public display of submission, humility, and commissioning. As Christ places himself in a humbling, submissive role to that of John the Baptizer, He is simultaneously being commissioned into the ministry. The voice in heaven that acknowledged Jesus' identity as the Son also validates His ministry by expressing pleasure in Him. It is as if God is saying: *this is my beloved Son and I am well pleased with who He is and what He is doing.*

There are people who engage in ministry without such a commissioning event, by doing so they cripple their ministry from being all that it could be. God desires to sanction your life and ministry in such a way that it validates who you are and to whom you belong. It also answers the "why" to the many situations you've found yourself in throughout your life that simply didn't make sense. Every minister needs a call, covering, and commissioning. Within most denominations, the concept of commissioning is displayed through a trial sermon and ordination process. During the trial sermon event God acknowledges our identity as ministers of the church. The church then accepts that acknowledgement or call as we enter into a time of preparation. After such time one is then commissioned.

This is the time that God uses to validate and support you by allowing you to find pleasure in your work. When people engage in ministry without these events in place they are working without the covenant of God and the church (the people of God). At the time of commissioning God sends the minister and the church receives the minister. If either element is missing then the ministry is problematic. Paul taught this in Romans 10:14,

> *"How then can they call on him who they have not believed? and how can they believe on him whom they have not heard? and how shall they hear without one preaching? And how shall they preach, except they be*

sent? as it is written, How beautiful are the feet of them that preach the gospel of peace, and bring glad tidings of good things!

The commissioning and validation of God and the Church is crucial for us as ministers because of the struggles that we must face in our work. Our model, the beginning of Jesus' public ministry, demonstrates this fact. Notice that immediately after the public announcement of Jesus Christ and his ministry, Jesus enters into a God-planned and initiated time of testing. Thus, whenever the Word of God is spoken, that Word must be proven through tests, trials and temptations. The moment God's Word was spoken of Jesus and his forthcoming ministry, the test began. For God's Spirit leads Christ into the wilderness to prove God's spoken Word over the life of Christ. This is no different in your life and ministry. If God has spoken into your life a word of ministry for others, it must be tested. So do not be shocked or disheartened, just walk into the wilderness. This period of testing is all part of God's plan to shape you into the minister you shall become.

The Spirit led Christ into the wilderness to endure this period of testing because it was all part of God's divine plan for Christ. The wilderness represents danger and struggle. It has been noted that apart from a few rugged people like John who made the wilderness between the Jordan Valley and Judean hills their home, most people viewed the wilderness as a dangerous and inhospitable setting. Even so, this horrible wilderness experience was in God's plan. Have you ever found yourself in places that were unpleasant, hostile and perhaps even dangerous? Often times these are the places where God situates you so that you can be made. Remember, don't fight it; walk in it. Remember that since this is part of God's Divine plan there are certain things that Christ can believe with certainty and so can we.

For instance, Christ does not have to panic or become frightened of the test because He knows that this is well-orchestrated and premeditated by God. Furthermore, he does not have to be concerned with his condition after such testing is complete. He knows that because God has designed the test, He has also appointed "the angels" that will come and minister to him (verse 11).

Brothers and sister, we must keep in mind that just as there is a set time for the test to begin, there is also a set time for the test to end. This temptation story, taken from the early public ministry of Jesus Christ, provides a prophetic vision of things to come for us as ministers. At the same time it instructs us in how to combat and defeat the enemy. When we view the temptation encounter from this perspective we can clearly see that this was no plan of the enemy, for Satan gains nothing and loses everything.

The testing, or temptation encounter, is one of the things that the enemy uses to sabotage the work of ministers. The enemy attempts to deceive people and make them believe that if they were really called of God things would immediately fall into place in their lives. In other words, the enemy is hoping that we will interpret a wilderness experience as a sign that God does not approve of our ministries, and therefore, abandon our work. The idea that only those ministers who are rich and appear to be stress-free are truly called of God, is a lie from the enemy.

Other people become overwhelmed with feelings of inadequacy during the wilderness experience, which causes them to develop a complex of inferiority and insufficiency. Well, the idea that we cannot accomplish what God has called us to accomplish by ourselves is true. Without God none of us could accomplish anything, especially anything good. In addition, no one is worthy of God's call, no, not one. Yet we can be assured that what is impossible to man is possible with God.

Remember that as a novice minister you will often find yourself in a wilderness state. While in this place of depression, fear, doubt and despair remain mindful that this is a test of God's will, plan, and call on your life. This test will ultimately act as a sign of vindication and validation of your ministry, providing you with the type of *road to Damascus* experience that is so desperately needed in a minister's life. Be careful to learn the lessons that God will reveal to you through your wilderness experience so that you can be molded into that which God has designed for you to become.

Oftentimes this pre-ministry wilderness experience is the young minister's first encounter with the ever-present nuisance known as the enemy. This initial battle with the Irritant One lays the framework for future battles yet to be played out in the remainder of this struggle called life. During this encounter and defeat of the enemy, one should develop a sense of faith that can continually be applied throughout the ministerial life.

Times of struggle present the best opportunities for ministers to sharpen their skills, develop their identity and build confidence. Be certain that if you are called to God's ministry, the enemy will attempt to stifle your work as much as possible. In actuality, you should be more concerned if you do not experience any opposition in response to your decision to pursue ministry. While Satan does not possess the ability to see into the future, he certain can deduce things in advance. The enemy's agenda is to eliminate you as a vessel of God before you have had time to fully mature into God's design.

We Wrestle against our Physical World

And after he had fasted forty days and forty nights, he was hungry. And then the Tempter came to him and said, If you are the Son of God, speak to these stones that they might become loaves of bread. But he answered and said, It is written, Man shall not live by bread alone, but by every word that comes out of the mouth of God.

The internal struggles of a minister must be waged against the physical world around us. You must first come to an acceptance and understanding of who you are as a person, before you can proceed to develop as a minister. It may seem like a simple concept, but it must be emphasized that before one can lead another, they must first know the way themselves. It seems obvious, but there are many ministers who operate outside of this order.

We often see people entering ministry without doing the hard of work of preparing themselves emotionally and spiritually. As ministers, we must come to grips with ourselves: our vulnerabilities, insecurities, uncertainties, desires, motives, lusts, and fears. All of these matters of life and identity come to the fore during a wilderness experience.

In the key text we are told that Jesus willingly fasted 40 days. Upon the completion of the fast he was *hungry*. What a powerful statement of the incarnation that the Creator of everything would position Himself in a posture of hunger, weakness and insufficiency. The question to ask is this: why did Christ allow Himself to be hungry. Perhaps this was done so that He could experience what we experience when we deal with our own humanity.

In order to truly deal with who we are as individuals we must deal with our own humanity. When listing the problems of our society and world it is obvious that we are grossly deficient and immensely incompetent for the task at hand. We wrestle with our limitations in view of our problems. Considering our inadequacies in comparison to the task before us is painful and intimidating. How dare we as ministers believe that we can change the world with our small, sinful, and feeble hands? Yet, God has called us to do just that work.

For Christ the position of hunger involved much more than physical hunger, it symbolized a position of lack and insufficiency of sustenance. It is important to understand the position of need and insufficiency because, like Christ, we are also called to minister to individuals that are in a position of lack. In order for ministers to truly minister to people who hurt, want and suffer, we must first experience these times of suffering ourselves.

Thus, it should come as no surprise to you that the lifestyle of ministry is not one of continuous affluence and prosperity. Just as God allowed Christ to experience the low parts of life, it is God's plan for ministers to experience suffering as well. The author of Hebrews wrote, in Hebrews 11:5, *"For we don't have a high priest that cannot understand and feel the feelings of our infirmities; but he was in all points tempted just like we are, yet without sin."* Christ understands us because He suffered as we suffer. It is a great lesson when ministers can encourage suffering people to hold on because they understand suffering, and what it means to hold on.

Furthermore a position of lack also strengthens our dependency on God. For it is only after we have been too far down to get up and too far gone to return home that we really see what God can do. It has been said that to receive a miracle one must be in a position to need a miracle. Before God can mold you into the minister that you shall become, God must first break you from the person that you have been. This process hurts and is very scary, but it is part of the wilderness experience that is so very necessary in development.

Notice that in the wilderness experience that Christ encountered, the tempter arrives right on schedule. This was no surprise to God, in fact, God allowed it. There are numerous stories throughout scripture where God allows His servants to go through struggles and tests that are meant to develop them. A good example occurs in 1 Samuel 17:34-37. This section of the Bible records the conversation of Saul and David prior to the Goliath encounter. Saul informs David of his inadequacies in relation to Goliath and David responds by recalling the wilderness experiences of his past. David informs Saul that he had killed a lion and a bear with his hands in times past, and he declares that this uncircumcised Philistine would suffer the same fate. God uses the events in David's past to give him the courage to combat Goliath in the present. Whatever trying event you may find yourself in today, consider it as preparation for what's to come in life.

Moreover, when the enemy arrives and he attacks the very words spoken by God, know that the attack is on God, not you. In our text of study God declared that *this is my beloved Son*. The enemy hears this declaration and, as always, attacks the very Word of God by saying, *if you are the Son of God*. Notice that it is the very Word of God, not the person, that is being attacked. The enemy attacks Jesus because of the Word of God.

Likewise, the enemy does not attack you because of who you are but rather because of what was spoken by God over your life and ministry. New ministers must remember that this resistance from the enemy is never a personal matter but always a prophetic matter. The enemy must attack you because of what God has declared that you will do and become. Consequently, it does not matter how you appear today or what you are doing now, if God has called you to great things, then there is a test and wilderness experience awaiting you. Remember that when Paul was called it was spoken over his life that he would have to suffer for the great calling he had received. *Acts 9:15...for he is a chosen vessel unto me, to bear my name before the Gentiles, and kings, and the children of Israel: For I will show him how he must suffer greatly for my name's sake.* Suffering is the prerequisite to greatness in God.

Upon further reflection of this encounter I remembered words from a preacher much more seasoned than I. His words were simple, "young preacher if you can keep your hands off of the sisters, keep them out of the plate and stay humble, you'll be a great preacher." These words correlate directly with the words of Saint John recorded in John 2:15-17.

> *Don't Love the world, neither the things that are in the world. If anyone loves the world, the love of the Father is not in them. For all that is in the world, the lust of the flesh, and the lust of the eyes, and the pride of life, is not of the Father, but is of the world. And the world passes away, and the lust with it: but the one that does the will of God abides forever.*

John's teachings parallel the story of the temptation of Christ. John provides a three-category approach in which all sin can be placed. While it would do well for all to avoid these categories of sin, this is especially important for those living out ministry. Note that the first category mentioned by John was the lust of the flesh (humanity). Also note that when the tempter arrives he tempts Christ with an appeal to the humanity, to eat. Every Christian should be aware that their human nature is not in line with the will of God for their lives. Neither is your humanity in line with your God-given ministry. Our reason for entering ministry is not to fulfill our physical desires, but to fulfill the God spoken Word over our lives. Once again, this is why ministers must check our motivations. John's words are still true today. What if God's desire for your ministry does not equate with your desire for your ministry? Be sure that lust is not intertwined with your goals for ministry and success.

After further investigation there appears to be yet another level of teaching present in our text. Henri Nouwen wrote in his book *In the Name of Jesus,*

> 'Jesus' First temptation was to be relevant; to turn stones into bread. Oh, how often have I wished I could do that! Walking through the 'young towns' on the outskirts of Lima, Peru, where children die from malnutrition and contaminated water, I would not have been able to reject the magical gift of making the dusty stone-covered streets into places where people could pick up any of the thousands of rocks and discover that they were croissants, coffee cakes, or fresh-baked buns, and where they could fill their cupped hands with stale water from the cisterns and joyfully realize that what they were drinking was delicious milk. Aren't we priest and ministers called to help people, to feed the hungry, and to save those who are starving? Are we not called to do something that causes people to realize that we do make a difference in their lives? Aren't we called to heal the sick, feed the hungry, and alleviate the suffering of the poor? Jesus was faced with these same questions, but when asked to prove his power as the Son of God by the relevant behavior of changing stones into bread, he clung to his mission to proclaim the Word and said, *One does not live by bread alone, but by every word that comes from the mouth of God.*"[xv]

Nouwen suggests that in ministry we are frequently faced with experiences of low self-esteem and inadequacy because we face problems in the lives of others that we do not have sufficient skills, finances, experience, training, knowledge or connections to solve. When looking at the ills of society it appears that we have been asked to move mountains with a simple dinner spoon. This feeling of irrelevance and inadequacy is commonplace among clergy in our post-modern society. If we possess a spirit of marginality and irrelevance it is very difficult to preach relevant messages, teach pertinent lessons and give applicable advice. So what are we to do?

It is here that we look at a training module that Christ allowed His disciples to experience. The story is recorded in Matthew the 14th chapter. It tells us that one day after Jesus taught the people he saw a great number of them and they were hungry. The Bible says that they did not have enough food or money to feed the people. Then Andrew brought to Christ a young man with five small barley loaves and two small fish. After Jesus organized the five thousand men, plus women and children, he did something remarkable. He blessed the meal and asked the disciples to distribute the meal to the people. Since there were five loaves and two fish equaling seven items of food, there would have been five disciples left with empty baskets.

The power of this story is that these men reached their hands into empty baskets and pulled out fish and bread. This miracle is a physical example of how ministry should appear. It is the faith to stand when you know that you are insufficient for the task; and yet you attempt it anyway in the Name of Christ. We are called to reach into the abyss of nothing and pull out a blessing for God's people. While you may feel that you can only do very little for the people you serve, you have been given the keys to connect people with God. When this connection takes place, great things happen.

This apparent power given to the followers of Christ must remain subject to the *will* of God. In our story Jesus is encouraged to use this power for personal gain as opposed to accomplishing the *will* of God. We must remember that Jesus did have the power to change the stones but this would not have been the *will* of God. In our society we see clergy daily abusing their power for their own political, financial, and even personal gain. Ministers have God-given power to influence and motivate people, as well as pray and change things.

Jesus declared in John 15.16 that we can ask anything of the Father and it shall be granted. What should we be asking for? As servants of the Lord we must remain focused on accomplishing the purpose for which we are called. The goal in the life of the minister is not to obtain as much *bread* as possible but to accomplish God's *will*.

Many people enter ministry because they are only privy to witness the public display of affection shown clergy. Sometimes people see the pastor's salary and anniversary package and decide to enter ministry as a lucrative vocation. This one-sided view of ministry conceals the darker side. My intent in discussing the wilderness experience is to present you with the truth so that you are challenged to call your motivations under subjection. It is my desire that you would be aware of the perks of ministry, but also aware of the pitfalls.

We Wrestle against our Perceptions of the World

Then the devil took him up to the holy city, and sat him on the highest peak of the temple, And said unto him, If you are the Son of God, throw yourself down: because it is written, He will give his angels orders concerning you: and in their hands they will hold you up, so that you won't hit your foot against a stone.

Jesus said unto him, It is written again, you shalt not tempt the Lord your God.

Our text takes us into the inner motivations of Christ's desire to accomplish the will of the Father. Ministers are to be reminded that we did not enter ministry for a Rolls Royce or Bentley, but so that God would be glorified through our obedience in life. In this section of the passage Christ is taken to the pinnacle of the temple to be propositioned. The enemy quotes the words of the Father, *if you are the Son of God,* and then interestingly enough begins to quote scripture. The Tempter quotes Psalms 91.11-12, *for he shall give his angels charge over you, to keep you in all your ways. They shall hold you up in their hands, so that you won't hit your foot against a stone.*

Of course the problem is that this quote is taken out of context, the meaning of the text is completely lost. The passage supports the idea that God has angels that protect His servants from danger, not that angels will uphold a test against the Word of God. God's angels are not here to enable us to jump in front of speeding automobiles or to wrestle lions, but this is the very absurdity of the request.

Yet another universal lesson to be taken from this text is that scripture can be used properly and improperly. As ministers of the Gospel it is imperative that we make every effort to properly interpret and handle the scriptures. One never wants to knowingly or unknowingly misuse or apply the text. This can cause serious and immense damage to the body of Christ.

Christ responds to the misuse of scripture by the enemy with an appropriate use of scripture. He quotes Deuteronomy 6:16 to refute the request of Satan. Christ's statements were appropriate for several reasons. First He directly addressed the temptation the enemy tried to initiate. It is wrong and impossible to tempt God. Second, Christ reaffirmed to the enemy that He was well aware of His identity and call. Christ informs satan that He is his God in this conversation. No matter what the enemy may plan, Christ is still God over him. This beautiful teaching should be rehearsed in the minds and hearts of ministers everywhere. We too have a special identity: servants, friends, even children of God. The next time you find yourself in the middle of a test, remind the enemy that you are still a child of God.

Furthermore this text also addresses a sane and proper acknowledgement of one's identity. A good friend once informed me that many ministers want to be a "wonder." That is to say that there is a desire within many to be a celebrity within the church; to be known for accomplishing the spectacular. The desire grows and they begin to want the things that others have received from the ministry.

John described this type of longing as the *lust of the eyes*—the sin that causes us to look at others and compare ourselves. This is the sin that almost caused the Psalter to slip in the 73rd number of Psalms. Ministers must stop believing that we are in competition with one another and understand that my calling and your calling can be different, similar and distinct all at the same time.

If you fail to eliminate this lust mindset it will ultimately warp your motivations and cause you to focus on things other than God's will and glory. When ministers actually begin to desire fame and fortune through their ministry, it means that they have forgeten that ministers are called to be servants.

When the mother of James and John approached Jesus about special recognition and appreciation in His kingdom, Jesus informed her that while these seats of recognition exist, they are only for those whom the Father has prepared them for. Then Christ tells the disciples, in Matthew 20:25, *"Don't you know that the princes of the Gentiles exercise dominion over them, and they that are great exercise authority upon them. But it will not be so among you: but whosoever will be great among you, let them be your minister; And whosoever will be chief among you, let them be your servant: Even as the Son of man came not to be ministered to, but to minister, and to give his life as a ransom for many."* We are called to serve God, God's people and the world around us—not to be famous.

Henri Nouwen wrote,

"The second temptation to which Jesus was exposed was precisely the temptation to do something spectacular, something that could win him great applause. *Throw yourself from the parapet of the temple and let the angels catch you and carry you in their arms.* But Jesus refused to be a stunt man. He did not come to walk on hot coals, swallow fire, or put his hand in the lion's mouth to demonstrate that he had something worthwhile to say. *Don't put the Lord your God to the test, he said."*

As stated earlier some ministers enter ministry for all the wrong reasons. Their perceptions are impacted by the things that they see. Often these same ministers are disappointed when their ministry does not develop as others have, or to the degree that they desire. This is all the restful of disillusioned perceptions.

Jesus was able to defeat the enemy during the temptation story because His perception was clear. The enemy took Christ to the Temple. The Temple represents the most respectable and holy place on earth. This is the very place where the Spirit of the Lord came to commune with the people. It was here that the enemy asked Christ to jump.

In that request he was asking Christ to show who He really was in the Father's house. How inappropriate this request sounds now, that Christ would jump off of the Temple, stealing the glory that is reserved for the Father for Himself. Imagine a grand display of angels appearing and enrapturing Christ to a position of safety, displaying Christ's true identity and providing Him the glory that He was due.

Jesus knew who He was and to whom He belonged. He also knew that this scheme was not of the Father. He was not tricked by this apparent appeal to be glorified by men. God had already honored him. Likewise, as ministers we must work to keep our perception clear and to maintain the right perspective. The truth is, most ministers will never pastor a church and even fewer will pastor a mega-church. Understanding the unique call that God has placed on your life and how God wants you to serve is the first step in developing a perspective of contentment.

We Wrestle against the Powers of the World

Again, the devil took him up into an exceeding high mountain, and showed him all the kingdoms of the world, and their glory; And said unto him, All these things will I give to you, if thou will fall down and worship me. Then said Jesus unto him, you get away Satan: for it is written, You will worship the Lord your God, and him only shall you serve. Then the devil left him, and, the angels came and ministered unto him.

Concerning the third temptation Nouwen writes,

"You all know what the third temptation of Jesus was. It was the temptation of power. *I will give you all the kingdoms of this world in their splendor, the demon said to Jesus.* When I ask myself the main reason for so many people having left the church during the past decades in France, Germany, Holland and also in Canada and America, the word power easily comes to mind. One of the greatest ironies of the history of Christianity is that its leaders constantly gave in to the temptation of power – political power, military power, economic power, or moral power – even though they continued to speak in the name of Jesus, who did not cling to his divine power but emptied himself and became as we are. The temptation to consider power an apt instrument for the proclamation of the Gospel is the greatest of all. We keep hearing from others, as well as saying to ourselves, that having power - provided it is used in the service of God and your fellow human beings – is a good thing. With this rationalization, crusades took place; inquisitions were organized; Indians were enslaved; positions of great influence were desires; Episcopal palaces, splendid cathedrals and opulent seminaries were built and much more manipulation of conscience was engaged in."

Pride is indeed the minister's worse enemy. It is a sin that tells us we ought to be more than we are. It robs the minister of contentment and distracts them from the will of the Father. As the Apostle John wrote, *the pride of life, is not of the Father, but is of the world. And the world passes away, and the lust with it: but the one that does the will of God abides forever.*

Satan is well aware of this sin for it was this sin that he fell under when he desired to be like God. So he offers Christ all of the splendor that this world has to offer, in hopes that Christ will also succumb to the lust of pride. Satan offers Christ all of the authority, wealth, and materialism of the world. How comical this offer seems to us. Why would Christ relinquish eternal glory in heaven for temporal glory on earth? But this is always what the enemy offers to us, an instantaneous fix that threatens our patient glorious reward. Ministers ought not sell themselves short settling for earthly praise and recognition. God's calling is higher than an earthly position or award. The ultimate goal can only be obtained once the good fight of faith has been fought and the race run with diligence. There is no instant way to fulfill God's calling on your life, one must live it out every day.

Get up each day and face the unknown with a sense of courage and confidence in your God-given gifts and purpose. Put all faith in God and stand sure that He will complete the good work that He has begun. Remember that when you feel all hope is gone and all is lost, God's ministering spirit will always come and revive your soul again. When selfish pride arises, remember your Heavenly reward. When loneliness comes, remember that this world is not your home and your calling is not to please the people of this world.

There may be times when God's calling forces you to separate from friends, or to preach and live messages that are not appealing to those around. You may even be called to stand against the very nation where you reside.

I beg of you not to grow weary during your journey. Be patient during your process of preparation and allow God to mold you into what He has in mind for you. Paul declared, *I charge you therefore before God, and the Lord Jesus Christ, who shall judge the quick and the dead at his appearing and his kingdom; Preach the word; be instant in season, out of season; reprove, rebuke, exhort with all long suffering and doctrine.*

3   THE PROCESS

BEING CERTAIN OF THIS VERY THING THAT THE ONE
WHO HAS BEGUN A GOOD WORK IN YOU WILL
CONTINUE TO COMPLETE IT UNTIL THE DAY OF CHRIST
JESUS
PHILIPPIANS 1.6

In order for us to fully mature in ministry and life we must have full confidence that we are in God's designed plan. Paul informs us that he was certain that the very one that began a good work with our lives was capable and able to continue the work until that appointed time of Christ's return or completion.

A great preacher once said I want to live my life in such a way that when I die I am completely used up. He wanted to pour out every creative, intelligent and good aspect of his being into others, and not take an ounce of what God had given him to the grave. What a bold expression of his desire to fully mature in ministry. These are the words of a man that recognizes that he does not have to know how each page of his life fits into the larger story. He just trusts God. Have you lived and matured enough to see how God works things out in your life?

I can vaguely recall the spring of 1997. I was in seminary and my closest friend, The Reverend Norris Lynn Jones, suggested that we complete a unit of Clinical Pastoral Education (CPE) together, at the local hospital. This internship would fulfill one of our graduation requirements. The only problem here was that I had no desire to work in the hospital. I did not see the value of such ministry. I was focused on completing my studies and I thought I was too good of a preacher not to get a church offer. I had a distinct and deliberate plan for my life but God had more in store for me.

Rev. Jones persisted and I agreed to enroll with him. I hated the experience from the beginning. Our CPE supervisor was a 70-plus-year-old white man and the other students were four middle aged white men. We constantly fought accusations of racism and I'm not certain if any good ever came into the patients' rooms.

It was not until several years later that I was able to reflect and see the learning that birthed in me through that experience. I realized that I was made to be a minister of the Gospel wherever people were suffering, not only from pulpits but from every aspect of our community. I learned then that if I had spent more time living instead of fighting God's plan, I would have gained even more from that experience. God brought this experience back in to my life many years later and it became a passion of mine. I am amazed at how God can bring people and situations into our lives even if the benefit of those connections is not revealed until years later. Has God ever made a connection in your life that you perhaps did not see the benefit of until several years later? This proves the sovereignty of our God.

So what is the process of maturity in faith? How does God mature us into who we are to become? I have a few ideas that I have developed over the years that can aid us on this part of our journey. First God is a God of the story. God uses narrative and parables to deliver truths. I recognize that God speaks through epistles and proclamations, but I also respect that God chose to introduce Himself to us through a story. It is through the stories of the Genesis accounts of the fall, the flood, the failure and the man of faith that we learn of God. The Exodus story teaches us the foundation of redemption and the Gospels flush out all the truths of God's love. Just as the Biblical story is important, God also uses our own life stories to teach us. Yes, your life is a story, a wonderful depiction of what God can do with a willing servant. There is much power and learning that can come about when we look at the "big" picture of our life and not just the individual events or scenes. To fully understand what God is doing through you one must learn to utilize the power of the story.

Narrative theory holds that we have the ability to reshape and retell our story. Have you ever noticed how the stories you tell change over time? Stories of shame and rejection once felt become masked by a slight ray of arrogance and pride five years later. Or perhaps what you thought was unbearable then, really seems sort of reasonable now. What power we have when used for our own development. I believe this is all part of God's process of maturation.

Look back over your life and try to recall your emotions connected to the most painful, or embarrassing, or shameful moments of life. Do you still interpret those situations in the same manner, or has God taught you something through the process? Just look at all the lessons you've learned or missed because you allowed or hindered God to teach you through time, experience and reflection. Perhaps the old idiom is correct that experience is the best teacher.

A second principle to grasp when maturing in life and ministry is the power of relationship. Life is a relational experience. From the moment we are born we are in one form of relationship or another. God speaks to us through relationships. God speaks to us directly at times, but also speaks to us through others. We have the ability to learn from the lives and mistakes of others along the way. It is only when we reflect upon all the information that we are gathering can we mature.

In the following chapters I want to look at Christian maturity and ministry as being interrelated theories of theology, spirituality and education. As I weave my theology and my understanding of spirituality into my educational process it challenges me to use my entire life as an opportunity to reflect, to grow and to learn. I want to explore how the theories of Experiential Learning, Relational Theology, and Social Learning Theory impact and guide our personal development and those around us. I have argued that being in relationship is foundational for effective growth and that your life is a story that demonstrates God's faithfulness and love. That story is meant to be passed along to others so they can learn for you and you from others.

4   THE RELATIONSHIPS

THEY WILL BE MY PEOPLE AND I WILL BE THEIR GOD
JEREMIAH 32.38

In Pentecostal traditions theology is usually transferred orally and through song. I vividly recall singing simply songs like *"take the Lord along with you everywhere you go"* and *"If you call on Jesus, He will answer prayer."* We would sing these up tempo call-and-response songs that had few words to them for what seemed to be hours at a time. The lyrics of these songs contributed to my theology of a living, present God interacting with me in my life. I learned in this atmosphere that the Spirit of God is always present and active. Even when we don't sense it, God is yet there and willing to get involved. God is always molding, creating, and shaping us through each life situation and relationship.

In my theology, relationship is the adhesive that connects my understanding and my experience, painful or otherwise. For example, in April 2013 my father died. Although my father is no longer with me, God has helped me to understand how our relationship can be used as inspiration for my ministry. My father was my model and teacher in life. In reflecting on my father I find further evidence that relationship is crucial to learning. I learned far more from my Dad than I will ever glean from all the books I have read. Still, the thing that I miss the most is my relationship. I did not learn from him because of what he said, I learned from him because of who he was to me. My dad allowed me to see him with all of his faults and strengths. He was open to me. He loved and supported me even when I made mistakes. Dad modeled good behavior and then allowed me to try things for myself. He was always there to listen to me, challenge me and chastise me, but most of all to love me. This is what I bring to my ministry: an intimate personal relationship of model behavior. In ministry I am open to allowing people to see me as I am. I am transparent so that I can use myself without allow my story to become the focus of the other's learning. In this manner both I and those around me can grow together. Godly leadership is honest and transparent.

My understanding of persons in relationship with God resonates with Thomas Jay Oord's presentation of Relational Theology. [vi] Relational Theology attempts to explain how God interacts with people through the experiences of their lives. God experiences the joys and pains of life with us. God is not sitting high in heaven and watching us live out the days of our lives on the largest television in the universe. This is not the case at all. God is involved, experiencing and feeling the situations we experience along the journey. Have you ever experienced great pain and wondered how God felt at that very moment? God hurts when we hurt and rejoices when we rejoice.

While I appreciate Oord's theory, he fails to account for the ways in which God and people are active in times of suffering. This is most important because it is during times of stress, pain and crisis that we learn the most about who we are and who God is. I use the teachings of James Cone and Black Liberation Theology to help me understand my role and God's activity when I have suffered in my life.[vii]

I find Oord to be much too passive regarding suffering, much like some in my Pentecostal roots, as though our role in suffering is simply to endure until God comes along to deliver. Cone has helped me to understand that while God delivers, I too play an active role through suffering for my liberation, growth and learning. Both God and I are active to bring about God's designed plan in my life.

We are called to actively wait on the Lord. At my local church I teach that our job is to provide God the opportunity to bless us. How have you, through your obedience, provided God the opportunity to birth a blessing in your life? Have you been so busy praying against the hardship that you refuse to experience the gloom of the cross with Christ, thus limiting the glory of the resurrection?

I now realize that my relationship with God is at the core of my existence. It is the core of all of my relationships and experiences. My perception changes when I acknowledge that whatever I'm experiencing, God is experiencing as well. I learned at the age of six, as I surrendered my life to the Spirit of God, that I was engaging in a relationship with God. I learned of God's love for me and I discovered that I was accepted by God and the church. This acceptance is validation—if you and I are worthy to receive salvation than we are worthy for God to invest in us through relationship.

The Bible presents many examples of how people first interacted with God through the formation of a relationship.[viii] In addition, throughout the Scriptures the different authors detail the activity and characteristics that demonstrate the relational nature of God. Thus, in my personal church ministry I pray and look for God's activity in others so I can assist them in learning to accept themselves, to connect with their emotions and to be engaged with a beloved community. One former ministerial student of mine once said that she fully embraced this way of thinking on the day that she learned of the death of her ex-husband.

The church gave her good pastoral care right then and there by allowing her space to grieve. Her church supported her while she sat in her emotions and encouraged her through her suffering. This demonstrates the power of interpersonal relationships as foundational to theology. My former student was able to reflect upon the God that loved her through the love she felt from those around her. She experienced ministry through relationship.

In the relationship between God and people, God is Creator. Importantly, God is not a detached Creator but One who is fully engaged and active throughout our lives. God is open to feeling and experiencing life with and through our relationship.[ix]

Relationships: Connections and disconnections

People are designed for connection; nevertheless, we often struggle in relationships with each other and with God. In fact, the Biblical narrative begins with Adam and Eve disobeying God and breaking the relationship. The original sin was a denial of relationship, community and covenant. People make their own choices and all of our decisions impact our relationship with God in some way. Yet, relationship is so important to God, that God is always ready to reconcile with us. What an awesome God we serve. As a minister I encourage people to be free to accept the gift of God's grace in relationship so they can encounter the true, ever-present, powerful, loving God.

The divine-human encounter that we experience through our relationship with God sustains us through times of struggle. Such was the case of a minister friend of mine who became distraught after the premature ending of her engagement. The breech in this relationship was so significant that it began to impact her relationship with God. She was forced to begin a journey to restore her relationship.

Here is how God used me to aid her in her growth and development. She was in need of spiritual reconciliation. I led her to reconnect to her purpose by returning to her faith tradition and her beliefs about the will of God for us. I assisted her in finding value in her being, which reconnected her to God. Together we explored her understanding of being a person first, and a minister second.

I let her sit in the pain of her confusion without trying to rescue her. But I never left her alone. I informed her that I was available, watching from a distance at times, but always ready to be present if I thought she needed me. I sought to be present in her life in a way that God is sometimes present in our lives. I have discovered that often time God is within reach but appears to be further for our growth. Through my gentle questions she discovered that her experiences, though painful, were all part of the divine purpose for her life. She was able to acknowledge that God was yet there even though she did not feel or sense a Divine presence.

Has the classroom of life also taught you the importance of your personal relationship with Christ? This has certainly been true for me. I recall that when I mourned the death of my first child through miscarriage, God was there. Although God did not show up in the way I wanted, God was present. Certainly God did not emerge and instantaneously remove all pain, anger or guilt, as I would have perhaps desired. Instead I experienced all of those emotions and while I felt totally alone at times, I see now that I was not totally alone, because God was with me.

Trust me, I felt abandoned, disappointed by God and angry at God. Yet, as I reflected upon this experience I saw the presence of God spiritually, emotionally, and even physically through the people that cared and expressed God's love for me. God was there weeping along with my wife and I. God's still presence in those moments of grief reminds me of my own quiet presence when my oldest daughter, Tiajah, received her immunization shots as an infant. I recall taking her to the doctor and playing with her as the physician prepared the shot. When the needle pierced her fragile skin, Tiajah looked at me and cried a cry that I had never heard from her before. Watching her in this confused, painful and abandoned state caused me to cry because I knew what she could not understand that this pain was for her own good. While yet in my pain I was well aware that her pain was necessary not only for her growth and development, but indeed, for her very existence.

Have you ever suffered and it turned out to be for your good? Can you see this principle in others and yourself? Isn't hindsight wonderful as we learn to follow and develop in Christ?

Ministry and Suffering

If you haven't gotten it by now, I believe that God is the God of the suffering. God enters our story and experiences the painful moments with us. The Exodus of the Old Testament teaches that God is concerned and involved with those that are hurting and suffering. We also see evidence of God's involvement in our lives through the death, burial and incarnation of Christ.[x] God comes down to earth, through Christ, so that He might have a more enhanced relationship with those of us that are hurting, afraid and suffering. This theme of liberation, as James Cone argues, is the central theme of the Gospel. Furthermore, emancipation is the overarching theme of the Bible.[xi]

I believe that our life experiences parallel the teachings of the Bible in that whenever we are suffering God is our active partner to help us endure. This type of relationship has elements of mutuality.[xii]

While we both share in experiencing the joys and sorrows our journey, I have come to realize that we most clearly see the presence of God during times of conflict and struggle.[xiii] Hence, suffering is necessary to accomplish our identity as ministers and to develop our relationship with God. I am not teaching that you have to go and create some form of trouble or pain in your world to get closer to the Lord. On the contrary, I am suggesting that you already have enough pain that you have experienced, and will experience, to complete the journey. You simply have to learn how to maximize what you experience.

Just as God comes along to experience and show us things in our life's journey, it is our task as ministers to come alongside others and help them discover truths in their life. In a much smaller sense, we mirror the relationship that we have with God with those that we serve. Our job is to remain open, assisting fellow believers in discovering and exploring the activity of God as they experience life. One such example of this relational pedagogy was with an African American Baptist female minister I mentored named Sharon. Here is how I assisted her in understanding her ministerial development.

Sharon had only been in ministry for a few years when I encountered her. As our relationship grew I intervened in her learning experience to assist her in reaching new truths in her life journey. Specifically, I showed Sharon her value as a minister by expressing my pleasure in her work. I also helped her to see the good ministry encounters she had with others. When she received this positive feedback she was able to acknowledge her God-given value and overcome the limitations that her community of faith places on women in ministry. In short others told her that she couldn't but God through me showed her that she could.

I entered into Sharon's teachable moment by modeling for her a different type of leader than she had traditionally encountered. Following my understanding of David Kolb's learning cycle; I provided for her an observable experience with a male pastoral figure. Next, I highlighted the good pastoral care she provided through my observations of her ministry. When she was able to say, "I did good," it confirmed for her that her gender was not a limit upon her calling and skill set.

Ultimately, Sharon was able to conceptualize her observations and organize her thoughts into a theological reflection paper on Christian leadership. Finally, she implemented her newly found understanding in her life and practice by finding a new local faith community. Sometimes new knowledge yields change.

While I am by no means a horticulturist, I do understand that a plant can only grow so large in a small pot. At a certain point the plant must be re-potted in a different environment to continue maturation. So it is with us as well. The continuation of your maturity may be connected with your willingness to be repotted. Has God ever had to remove you from your surroundings to reveal certain truths to you? Are you willing to be repotted?

Belonging and Identity in Ministry Relationships

My faith culture and community informs me that I am

"somebody" or "someone" special simply because God created me. Since God created me, I am connected to God, come from God and shall return to God. As a young boy I remember singing, *"I'm blessed because God says I'm blessed…I am what God says I am."* My value, identity, and personhood rest in the knowledge and connectedness of my Creator. Every person created by God has value, dignity, worth, beauty, creativity, intelligence and personhood because they are etched in the image of God. Thus, my worth is not measured by others, nor by my intellect, but by my value, love and worth to God.

This philosophy of divine worth and personhood has been present and vibrant in the black church for generations. It was foundational in the struggle of the civil rights movement and in my own personal development. Rooted in the struggles of the African American experience for me is a great sense of pride and confidence.

When I reached Taylor University, however, I was told that my culture, religion and thus self were inferior to that of my white peers. Professors were quick to point out that my African American Pentecostal tradition was primitive. Yet, I was never comfortable with this "white is right" philosophy.

For me, strength was found in the knowledge that I received from my community that I was good enough for God and them. That sense of acceptance by God and community gave me the courage to continue with my studies and obtain my degrees.[xiv] It was wrong for certain professors to use their power over me and subject me to statements of inferiority and racial prejudice.

My college experience reminds me to be mindful of the issue of authority and power that exist between ministers and people. I am cautious not to use the influence that I have as a minister to abuse, belittle, or harm people in any way. Certain professors at Taylor taught me the damage that arrogance can do when possessed by people in authority. This destroys relationship. Thus, I am ever mindful to remain open to other people's respective family of origin, culture and heritage, especially when they differ from my own.

Belonging and identity are important factors in our spiritual development that impact the relationships. One of my goals in life and ministry is to assist and support people while allowing them to discover a realistic understanding of their own self-identity through experience-based learning.

In pastoral care it is very important that caregivers know who they are and how they function before assisting others with the crises of life. Thus, effective ministers have all wrestled with that big question in life: who am I. The answer to this question must be discerned and realized within the self.

I have come to an understanding of who I am by looking at my inner self as I remain in conversation with others. I am a black man living in two cultures and two worlds. I live and identify with the African American community of Detroit with all of its complications. I live in this world as a pastor, prophet, preacher father, husband and son. For many years I have also come to realize that I exist in a white world as well. This double consciousness plays out in my spiritual formation as well.[xv]

My father taught me to perform for my African American

culture so that they would be proud of me, and to produce for the white culture to prove myself and culture. Both worlds have become part of who I am. To be void of one would render a person that is not me. To be fully who I am I need both parts of myself.

As a minister, I know that in order for others to become effective they need to develop their own self-identity. Healthy self-identity encompasses all of the apparent cultural shame and pride that people carry with them and brings them to a place of wholeness within themselves. This is a place of understanding that affirms: God created me in His own image and likeness thus giving me value and purpose in life. This place of grace aids people in asserting that God loves them and that they are important to God and to others. Do you know who you are to yourself? Do you know who you are to God? Only after these two have questions have been tested and tried can you be comfortable with how others see you.

I once had a fellow chaplain minister at the hospital tell me a story of two doctors that embarrassed him in front of a family. The physicians spoke to him as though his presence and opinion did not matter. They dismissed him publicly. As he told me the story I said, "Wow, they really did not value you at all did they. I guess they did not think much of you and your ministry."

The minister erupted in anger towards me. He expressed his fury to me and refused to continue the discussion. I let him be mad because I was comfortable with who I was and what I brought to the table. I have also had doctors belittle me, and others refuse to take another step in the plan of care without my input. Since I am comfortable with who I am, I always strive to walk with a measure of confidence no matter what the other person may think of me. Once you have a sane assessment of who you are in God, it does not matter who you are to others. Have you come to know your strengths and limitations in God with regards to your personhood and ministry? How did you learn that lesson?

As stated earlier I get my value and worth from God. I believe that ministers must know that they and those they serve have value and worth to God too. In reflecting on the importance of self-identity and self-worth for ministers, one former student in particular comes to mind.

Mary was a second unit student that came to us from a different CPE program. She was terrified about presenting her material to the group. She felt that whatever she presented was not good enough and she kept belittling and degrading her work. She was hurt and afraid; thus, she was not developing as a minister or person. It took much nurture and support from me and her peers for Mary to see that she had value to offer the group. Not only did I support her but I also confronted her throughout the unit when I saw her returning to old behaviors of belittling and degrading herself. By the end of our time together I was able to guide Mary in breaking through her limitations and she changed her behavior. In order to assist a minister like Mary, who is saddled with shame, we must work to establish bonds of trust, nurturing, and constructive challenge.

Despite my or any minister's best efforts, not all people will respond in kind. For example, I once encountered a student, Tom that resisted the process from the beginning of the CPE unit. Two weeks into the unit he became aggressive and verbally belligerent to other members of the staff. Tom was not willing to reconcile the relationships that he broke. Without reconciliation there can be no liberation or freedom, and thus no learning.

I confronted Tom and he acknowledged that he saw no good that could come from the process or my confrontation, and was not willing to do the emotional work needed to grow and be successful. Indeed, people will not always see the value in the painful process of learning from heartbreaks. It is possible that, just as I struggled to see the beauty in an unfinished painting, some people will not understand the value of reflecting upon their life experiences until the end of the process. Have you grown to the place where you can see opportunity for growth in every situation? Have you ever seen others fail to grow because they were too stubborn to learn?

We're all Spiritual, We're all Connected

Spirituality is what connects us. We are all spiritual beings, God created us this way. Every human being has been created by God with the complexity of their personality and given a measure of spirituality. This is the ability to decide for oneself what is beautiful, holy, sacred, special or important. This is why everyone gives meaning, purpose and value to something. Just as beauty can only be seen once it takes on tangible form, your spirituality must also be demonstrated in your life.

As a minister I help people see their spirituality, meaning, purpose and value, whatever it may be. I have lived this value in that in my presence and person I have offered people of the different faith traditions and cultures a safe place to grow and learn.[xvi] I strive to be an intercultural minister.[xvii] That is to say that I am aware of my own culture and that of others, so that I can fully engage others in their culture without losing my own identity. I believe that God is big, much bigger than any one culture can define. God is active in more ways than one and it is to our benefit to appreciate the presence and activities of God in those not like ourselves. I have come to understand and see the value of experiencing God in other cultural manners and customs. Through these experiences I am able to better understand how all of people are connected.

5   THE CLASSROOM OF LIFE

I WANT TO KNOW CHRIST--YES, TO KNOW THE POWER
OF HIS RESURRECTION AND PARTICIPATION IN HIS
SUFFERINGS, BECOMING LIKE HIM IN HIS DEATH
PHILIPPIANS 3.10

It's Sunday morning and the pews are packed in this predominantly African American church. The saintly mothers are dressed in white while the elderly men are all in dark suits. The children, some asleep, are dressed in their Sunday best. The preacher is preaching and there is a feeling and a sound that is difficult to describe in words. The sound rhythmically bellowing from the Hammond B-3 organ is in cadence with the voice of the preacher as she masterfully intertwines ancient doctrinal truth and the modern struggles of survival in everyday black life in America.

One can almost taste and see the excitement, like smoke, hovering in the air as her voice crescendos ever so much higher and stronger with each point, as she prepares for the emotional and dramatic close of the sermon. The preacher artfully displays the skill of delivery with confidence, presence and spirit. Life experiences have given her a boldness that make her points much more poignant. The congregation cannot help but to be drawn into this powerful display of reason and emotion. For we believe that she has lived what she preaches. We cannot help but become enraptured in the moment as we observe the integration of experience, conceptualization, reflection, and experimentation. I love powerful worship encounters like these, and I have gleaned lessons from them through my observation in ministry.

As I reflect over my 25 plus years of being a minister and educator in the black church tradition I see the roots of my education theory of life. Though these experiences are vastly different from one another, the principles of learning are similar. Learning comes from observation, experience and reflection. After the death of my father in April 2013, amidst my grief and sadness, I discovered that I had learned more from my Dad than from any of my professors in undergraduate or seminary studies. I recognize now that he, along with my culture, were the two greatest influences on my learning, self-awareness and development. Based on this discovery I have come to the following conclusions about learning and ministry.

Learning as Spiritual Discipline

To be effective in ministry we must learn the lessons that God will teach us. God has established that learning takes place through the reflection of life experiences that occur in relationships with self and others. This relational-based, experiential learning fits well within the action–reflection model of adult learning theorists.

We are allowed the opportunity, through real-life situations, to explore both who we are as people and pastors, and how we relate to others to whom we are connected. I am continuously learning, and thus changing, through ongoing reflections of my life experiences. Albert Bandura's work on the importance of observation, self-efficacy and desired outcomes as motivation in human behavior and learning has been central to my understanding of self-reflection.[xviii] While I agree with Bandura's principles, I find that he places far too much emphasis on modeled behavior with regards to observation and imitation. Recognizing that learning is much more than observing and doing, I call on David Kolb's theory to complete what Bandura lacks in the cycle of learning.

In Experiential Learning Theory Kolb stresses that learning is "the process whereby knowledge is created through the transformation of experience. Knowledge results from the combination of grasping and transforming experience."[xix] In other words, learning does not only occur through observed experience, but also through the reflection of developing ideas and he reapplication of new concepts to subsequent experiences. Hence learning is a constant succession and we are continually being modified and recreated based on the previous and ongoing experiences of the learner.[xx]

Learning is conceived in a conflict and tension filled cycle of Concrete Experiences (CE) and Abstract Conceptualization (AC) juxtaposed with Reflective Observation (RO) and Active

Experimentation (AE).[xxi] People observe and reflect upon concrete experiences (life), then develop abstract concepts from which new implications for action can be derived and tested. When this cycle is complete, learning has taken place and the student carries this new awareness into another experience.

When I think of the ministers I have had the honor of supporting in the cycle of learning, Diane comes to mind. She had been in ministry for some time when we met. Diane's story was full of stubborn insistence and conflicting impulses most noticeably seen in her eight previous marriages. Her behavior was a maladaptation of her inability to deal with the shame she experienced in her parental relationships.

Diane's desire to hide, due to the shame, was evident in her interactions with others—she kept her distance and avoided forming meaningful relationships. I perceive that Diane's maladaptation of impulsivity and recklessness hindered her from reflecting upon her past experiences and eventually stunted her personal growth. I guided the student through the process of self-reflection by encouraging her to explore how her impulsive decisions and distant relationships prohibited her from developing trusting pastoral relationships. I asked her to reflect upon how her ministry was impacted by the fact that she remained distant from others.

Can you see how Diane's relationships and experiences hindered her ability to reflect and learn? Now consider your own life. In what ways could your ability to learn and develop be hindered? How can you actively remove those hindrances?

One of the reasons I challenged Diane to reflection on her past and present relationships is because relationships play a crucial role in learning. In this matter I look to the principles of Relational Theology for theoretical support. As stated earlier, I understand that God has created people and called us to be in relationship with God, others and even ourselves so that we may learn and grow. Experience is never distinct from the people, culture and setting surrounding it. Hence, experience and relationship work together to create learning opportunities.

We see this connection illustrated in John 1.39 when Jesus told the disciples "to come and see" if he were the Messiah. Christ provided an environment that was conducive to building trust, transparency and connecting relationships.[xxii] Without connection, our relationships become weak and our ministry becomes less effective.

Parker Palmer wrote, "Good teachers (ministers are teachers) possess a capacity for connectedness. They are able to weave a complex web of connections among themselves, their subjects and their people so that the people can learn to weave a world for themselves."[xxiii] I have experienced that power of connection many times in ministry. For example, because I work to build trustworthy relationships, other people often feel comfortable confessing their most intimate secrets to me.

I recall one incident when a man called me to share his feelings of guilt and shame after viewing inappropriate sexual material on the internet. He expressed that because I had been so open with him, he felt he could trust me with such information. So you see, trust is critical for establishing relationships and creating a learning environment in which others feel comfortable enough to be vulnerable.

Trust is developed through the minister's willingness to experience newness. In my ministry, I encourage people to be open to new ideas, relationships, emotions, concepts and people. Understanding that change and newness are often terrifying to people, I am intentional about leading by example. At the beginning of every ministerial helping relationship I listen to people's stories and connect with them on the most basic human level as they share their fears and passions.[xxiv]

In addition, I affirm their giftedness and seek to encourage them in their growth areas. I challenge them to engage fully with their peers and I reveal myself to them, in moderation, in order to model transparency. These efforts allow for a relationship of trust to form between myself and those that I serve.

As a minister it is not my responsibility to control the people that I serve, but to create a relatively safe place for learning; a place where they feel free to experience and observe modeled behavior through relationships without fear of retaliation or abuse.[xxv] It is also not my goal to be liked by the people, but rather to be real with them by nurturing, challenging, and connecting with them for the purpose of growth in their pastoral skills and abilities.

Environment and Learning

Several other factors including previous behavior, cognitive/internal aspects, and environment/community impact a minister's learning. Bandura refers to this concept as "reciprocal determinism" and proposes that there is a causal relationship between a person's environment and their behavior. Behavior affects environment, and environment affects behavior.[xxvi] People are neither driven totally by inner forces nor completely and automatically shaped and controlled by their environment or culture. Instead, we function as contributors to our own motivation, behavior, and development within a network of reciprocal relationships and influences.

Culture, environment and/or community are substantial elements in our learning. If a safe environment and safe relationships provide a positive culture for learning, the opposite is also true that a fearful, dangerous, and unsafe environment limits learning. Very few people possess the self-efficacy to learn and grow in unsafe environments and relationships.

We see the dark side of learning and environment when we consider marginalized populations. Jawanza Kunjufu, a researcher, has spent his life and career studying the ills afflicting the black population in the United States. Primarily he observes the educational system and the issues impacting young black men. His work shows that even the best efforts made in the classroom setting are tremendously impacted by other elements of influence, namely community, home environments, economic status, media, and entertainment.[xxvii] Kunjufu's studies among others, support Bandura's theory that culture highly influences the education process and can either support or hinder learning.

Here I use the terms culture and environment interchangeably. Our environment provides much of the models we use to interpret the world, and conditions the way we learn. Culture provides the framework, rules and boundaries by which we all express ourselves and learn to function.[xxviii]

The culture that has influenced my learning consists of several layers of role models including parents, teachers, ministers, the African American Pentecostal Church, Black culture on the West-side of Detroit, the guys and girls in the neighborhood, gangs, and classmates. All of these elements have contributed to my conditioning. My understanding of, and learned behavior towards, police officers, teachers and illegal drug dealers were shaped and formed through my experiences and reflections in that culture.

In order to better understand how each of my students will approach their own ministry, I often look for their reflections and attitudes regarding public affairs and world events. One of my former ministerial student's was a Native American retired police office. One day I facilitated a group discussion about the Ferguson shooting of Michael Brown. I encouraged open dialogue and used this real life situation to compel the class to connect with both head and heart. It was very interesting to hear Joe express his concerns regarding the officer in question, whom he believed was misunderstood. Joe's culture and experience from being an ex-police officer shaped the way he interpreted the culture of frustration with police officers within the African American community.

Tension filled the room each student expressed their feelings, derived from their respective cultural backgrounds. Although the group did not totally agree, they were willing to cordially disagree with one another. They connected to each other by recognizing their own cultural perspectives within themselves and those of other students.

Now think about how you might have handled yourself in the previously described conversation. Have you carefully though about how your cultural background influences your life and ministry? To what extent are you able to manage peaceful disagreements with people who do not share your cultural background? Do you select friends that will foster a holy environment for your spiritual growth? As you reflect on your entire being, including your relationships and environment, you will begin to see the plan of god for your life and ministry.

6   THE LESSONS

DON'T BEHAVE LIKE THOSE IN THIS WORLD BUT LET
GOD TRANSFORM YOU INTO A NEW PERSON BY
CHANGING THE WAY YOU THINK.
ROMANS 12.2

God teaches us lessons through different kinds of experiences.
Will you be prepared to receive your lesson when it comes?

Perhaps the most dramatic and personality shaping event in my
life thus far has been the death of my father. Through this single
experience I was thrust into a crisis moment of epic proportion. My
identity, meaning, purpose and individuation were all at stake. My
father's life and death have shaped who I am. When I consider my
relationship with him, it becomes clear that the good and bad days,
joys and sorrows, ups and downs have all shaped my personhood and
ministry. For we become who we are meant to be through wrestling
internally within ourselves and externally with others.

At the core of my understanding of ministry is the belief that all
people are born with a Spirit, a purpose, and great potential, all given

by God. God designed our Spirit to be the essence of who we are and is separate from, though influenced by, our environment, relationships and life experiences. As we reflect on our experiences we can identify the patterns and behaviors that make up our personalities. I see evidence of this truth everyday as I observe the growth of my two teenaged daughters.

Although my daughters are only two years apart in age, they are significantly different in personality and spirit, and therefore respond differently to the same situations.

Crisis moments provide a unique opportunity for development and maturity. I believe that God permits these moments to take place in our lives so that our personhood and ministry may be developed. Hence, your ministry will mature as you reflect upon the experiences, relationships and past choices in your life. If you ever questioned the importance of taking the time to reflect on how your past experiences shape your personality, this chapter will prove that your doubts were unfounded. Ministry and personhood are intricately intertwined.

Erik Homburger Erikson is the theorist most influential in my understanding of personality and ministerial development. Erikson argues that we are all engaged in a life-long developmental process facilitated by conflicts. Let's begin to dig deeper by exploring Erikson's bio-psychosocial theory: *ego identity*.

Erikson's understanding of ego is similar to my understanding of the Spirit. I understand ego identity as the conscious self that people develop through relationships and experiences. According to

Erikson, the ego develops as it successfully resolves crises that are distinctly social in nature. Such crises involve establishing a sense of trust in others, developing a sense of identity in society, and helping the next generation prepare for the future.

The ego identity, or spirit, is constantly changing through new experiences in conflictual situations and relationships. The spirit is a delicate matrix shaped by life experiences, internal elements like genetics and ego, and external elements such as community, family, and culture.[xxix] Each individual's behavior is connected to their crisis moments in life.[xxx] These crisis moments are used by God to shape our Spirit, which in turn shapes our ministry.

Sometimes our crises moments grow beyond single instances and become year-long struggles. Such was the case of Linda, a 60-year-old African American female that I counseled as a pastor. When I met Linda she was a recent widow and she served as a caregiver for several members of her family, including her recently deceased husband. I perceived, using Eriksonian language, that Linda's conflictual issue was one of *Identity verses Role Confusion*.

Linda's behavior was the product of low-esteem, diminished goals, and her inability to say no when others made demands of her. Hearing Linda's story reminded me of my own relationship with my father. After his death I grew to understand that so much of my identity was connected to his idea of who I should be.

Although the growth process was not easy, I can now restructure my perception of my identity according to my own desires and goals. As a pastor I helped Linda by empowering her to see the need to say "no" to her daughter's demands of constantly babysitting her granddaughter. I encouraged her to pursue her goal of obtaining a graduate level theological degree and become a certified chaplain. With my support Linda released herself from the need to be everything to everybody, and she enrolled in seminary and continued to Clinical Pastoral Education.

Development is Progressive

Personality and spiritual development are *epigenetic* in nature, meaning that these processes occur through a lifelong learning process.[xxxi] This process entails both the interpersonal and cultural needs of the individual. Each stage has its own crisis incident and presents the individual with tasks to be achieved and learning to be acquired.

Furthermore, each stage builds upon the successful completion of earlier stages.[xxxii] The earlier crises become foundational strengths or growth areas for the later crises, and those not successfully completed are expected to reappear as a future crisis. If you do not learn from your experiences, you are doomed to repeat them until you learn the lesson.

I was reminded of the *epigenetic* nature of development when Christine joined my Clinical Pastoral Education class. I perceived early in the unit that Christine was wrestling with shame issues. Christine's shame crisis caused her to display socially disconnected behavior. She persistently avoided conversing or sharing with peers after group sessions.

Christine's struggles with shame emerged in young adulthood. Her relationship with her parents was plagued by pain, anger, and rejection because they disapproved of her love interest. Christine's struggles caused her to "run away" from adult intimate relationships; she was unwilling to engage emotionally. The mean and cruel reactions of her parents kept resurfacing in her life, and she had been unable to disassociate from the shame.

Christine expressed to me that she lived a "lonely life." As a minister I asked her to acknowledge her anger towards her parents. I challenged her to trust those around her and to become open to developing real relationships within the group, church and hospital staff. Although this level of social connection made Christine uncomfortable, I believed it was the only way for her to develop a positive image of her pastoral skills. With support, Christine eventually generated the courage to let people into her world and began to attend social functions when invited.

Now consider your own personal and Spiritual development. Have you ever noticed that certain traits and lessons keep resurfacing in your life? Are you willing to identify the patterns and do the emotional work of releasing this baggage?

While internal reflection is important, it is not enough. Social relationships are also key to developing the ego or Spirit. Jean Baker Miller's Relational Cultural Theory (RCT) affirms that all persons drive towards connections, relationships and acceptance. [xxxiii] Furthermore, RCT holds that connections are important and that *disconnections* are the main cause of mild and severe psychological and spiritual problems that diminish the development of ministers. Disconnections include all levels of broken relationships, from being ignored to all forms of abuse. I see disconnection as conflicts.

There are several reasons why conflict and disconnections exist between people. RCT proposes that one reason for conflict is the Central Relational Paradox. Since we all have a desire to be in relationships, and in said relationships all long for acceptance, there are things about ourselves that we deem unacceptable or unlovable. We often hide these things that we deem unlovable in an effort to keep them out of our relationships. This solution only creates more problems, because when we alter ourselves we cannot foster authentic, real or mutual connections with others. Thus, we must recognize that since we all come from God and are loved by God, we are free to be honest about our true identity.[xxxiv]

Another contributor to broken relationships, according to RCT, is negative relational images. *Relational images* are expectations that we each create out of our own past experiences in relationships. The inner pictures of what has happened to us in past relationships are developed as we simultaneously create a set of beliefs about the current state of our present relationships. Relational images thus determine our expectations not just about what will occur in future relationships but also about a person's understanding of herself or himself. Ultimately, relational images form the unconscious frameworks of our personality development.[xxxv]

We all have learned relational images. As a minister I help people discover the relational images that impact their interactions with others. Judith Jordan proposes that one way to discover our relational images is by completing the following statement, "When I am _____, the other person will _____".[xxxvi] I have used this model repeatedly when counseling individuals who are suffering from a breakdown in their relationships.

For example, John came to me because he was having problems connecting with his wife. He avoided sensitive issues because of his fear of rejection. The strains in his relationship also affected his ability to serve people as a minister.

When allowed to explore his disconnection John acknowledged that he believed that if he was actually honest about his feelings in his relationship, his wife would disconnect from him. John answered the paradigm as such, "When I am *emotional* people shut down and pull away from me." This thought was based on his relational image. John's image, based on relationships within his family of origin, was that people shut down when they become emotional.

My task as a minister was to challenge this relational image. I acknowledged John every time he became slightly emotional in our sessions together. Through this experience John recognized that the emotional connection developed in our counseling sessions had brought us closer in our relationship, not further apart. As I shared with John he began to see the value of connecting with his emotions, and he was able to reshape his relational image. He then reflected upon and tested his new theory with his wife and others he served. Gradually, John completely changed his image of the use of emotions in relationships and replaced it with a more positive image.

The truth is we all carry images, hurts, fears, and excitement from past relationships. This baggage will not fit under the rug. We must explore it. It is especially important in ministry that we encourage others to explore their own growth consciousness. The following five sections detail the concepts that I have found to be most effective in supporting the Spiritual development of others.

Ego Identity in Ministry

First, I listen carefully to each individual's story so that I can experience the conscious self that has developed through their relationships and experiences. I believe that our identities are shaped by the accounts of our lives found in our stories or narratives. As a minister I hone in on how people describe their story and help them to connect and identify their emotions.[xxxvii] Through this process people address the internal emotional conflicts of their lives.

For example, when I learned that one particular person had been through numerous marriages, I asked her to name the emotions that she associated with the concept of marriage. Through exercises like this, and prayer, people begin to see themselves as God sees them. Their identity becomes clear, not as a conquering lion, but as a willing servant. This is the most powerful form of self-identity. It is only when we see who we really are and how weak we really are that we can see the true strength of God.

Epigenetic Nature in Ministry

As a minister, I also listen to people's stories to ascertain what developmental crises maybe re-emerging at their current point in their life. Adult development is built upon childhood and adolescent experiences, so I allow people to return to past times in their life to look for patterns of behavior. When we connect the dots we see a clear picture of how God has been active in their development. We can also assist them in making decisions in their present situation.

Have you ever wondered why people seem to make the same poor decisions over and over again? Perhaps you have even found this to be true in your life. The truth is that until we have reflected to discover the patterns of our spirit (personality) and decided to do differently, we will repeat counterproductive patterns. The epigenetic cycle can only be broken when we decide to be different than we have been in the past.

Authenticity and Mutuality in Ministry

I look for other's ability to be authentic and vulnerable in my ministry relationships. In order for me to encourage such an open attitude, I must first model authentic behavior by being open and transparent. Openness also extends to learning and development. If one displays an attitude of *already knowing* everything this will be challenged as being unacceptable and not conducive to learning. Are you mature enough to acknowledge what you don't know? Are you willing to learn?

Connections and Disconnections in Ministry

Connectedness and Disconnectedness in ministry are other important aspects of development. As I work with people I consider the mutually empathetic and empowering relationships that they have developed during their life. Such relationships demonstrate an individual's ability to connect. I also consider relationships where disappointments, misunderstandings occurred because these demonstrate how an individual handles disconnection. Using this information I assist others in making links between their past and their present. I use family diagrams to look for reoccurring behavioral traits so that the individual may discover hidden personality traits. I challenge others with the following questions: Are there certain types of people that you have difficulty connecting with? If so, why? Are there certain types of people that you love to connect with? If so, why? What do you look to gain from your friendships? What are you seeking from others?

Conflict in Ministry

Conflict is inevitable in ministry and development. Some people strongly resist this means of reflective learning, because conflict makes them uncomfortable.[xxxviii] I challenge you not to run from conflict, but to remain open to what you might learn. A minister sister of mine, Krystal, struggled with this very issue of running from a painful past. An incident from her childhood that she had worked hard to bury reemerged when she found herself struggling to counsel a friend's mother whose son had committed suicide. Through our relationship I discovered that she had experienced the loss of a close loved one due to suicide herself, and in an effort to be "strong" for her family, she did not reflect and learn from that experience. Thus,

Krystal's growth was hindered and her ability to minister effectively to this new family was limited.

I heard Krystal's quiet voice and acknowledged her pain. I engaged her by expressing my sorrow for her cousin and displayed my empathy through voice, posture, touch and allowing for use of time. After establishing our mutual impact and connectedness, I encouraged Krystal to seek further grief work regarding her authentic self and pain. I also explored the wounded healer notion of experiencing grief with her, and encouraged her to connect to others while grieving.

Although she initially resisted, I explained to Krystal that she had to face this painful and demonic experience from her past, no matter how much if frightened her. As you reflect on your own life, are there some situations you are still running from because of fear?

7 THE COURAGE TO BE

BUT NOW O LORD, YOU ARE OUR FATHER; WE ARE THE
CLAY, AND YOU ARE OUR POTTER; AND WE ALL ARE
THE WORK OF YOUR HANDS.
ISAIAH 64.8

It takes courage to be who and what God has created you to be.
Most of us live life trying to be what we think others would have for
us or desire for us to be. How liberating it is, to simply accept who
you are according to God's plan. After all, that is your true self as a
person, minister and servant without any mask, or titles or any
imposed identity.

A very significant pain and most effective learning experiences
of my life's journey occurred several years ago. This event sums up
my understanding of a God that is living life with me. In my life story
I had developed a desire at a very young age to serve God as a
minister. I had given my best to understanding both God and people,
and to becoming the best minister I could be.

I had been living for a call from the church of my youth. I had prepared myself cognitively, emotively and spiritually for the charge. I was so certain that I heard the voice of God calling me to this particular church that I made great sacrifices to prepare for those holy orders. All things were in place and I received confirmation of said call. Then the unthinkable happened. Someone within church hierarchy pulled the rug out from under me. The charge was taken away and I was left to question my calling, purpose and life. The details of who said what are no longer important. There is no need for me to analyze what man was threatened or what woman had ulterior motives. I no longer care who liked me nor had issues with my walk, shape, and color or preaching ability. For me the question became where was God and how this could be a part of God's plan. Is God's plan for my life and ministry truly controlled by the feeble hands of mere men and woman? Or did God allow and even plan such events to play out in my life?

During this time of pain and embarrassment I looked back over my life and ministry in an attempt to understand what was happening to me. I determined that I would hold fast to the things that I believed. I wanted God to be glorified in everything that I encountered in life. I decided to live every day with a measure of dignity and pride in who I was in God so that I could stand up right before my family, friends, and enemies. I was determined to take this negative energy and use it to bring about something good. This magnificent struggle was the turning moment when I began to understand that if I was going to be like God that I must act like God even in painful circumstances. Thus I have endured much pain in order to develop the courage to be like God.

I now understand that in reflecting God's glory to the world with my life and ministry, I am to interact with the world in the same fashion that God engaged this world oh so long ago. All of my life and experiences guided me to engage with my surrounding world just as God did.

The final lesson in this book explains how to live out your God given purpose and calling in life and ministry, especially when unforeseen tensions arise. Since we have accepted Christ we have been instructed to do God's will and to be a man or woman of God, but what does that look like? What does a successful life look like according to God's standards? With few teachings on the subject, many people are left confused and waiting for a miraculous earth-shaking encounter with God to show them the next step to take, when they should already be living out their ministry.

We see this epidemic of aimless living displayed through a generation of young Christians that have no clue as to who they are and what they are called to be. This type of confusion moves me as a pastor, and thus I have been led to share seven characteristics that can be used as a guide to those who are drifting through life and ministry. Each concept is based in the nature of God as recorded in Genesis 1.1-5. I have applied these characteristics to my own relationships and experiences and offer them up as insight on how to discover one's purpose and ministry.

First let's begin with the obvious, you must be a believer that has surrendered your goals, purpose, aspirations, and will over to that of our God. You must develop and possess the qualities and characteristics of a Christian. In addition, you must recognize that we are created in God's image, and therefore we possess some of the same characteristics that God possesses. Since God is a Spirit and is not continually housed in a physical home, we are not created in His image wholly physical. Yet, there is a Spirit part to our being. *God is a Spirit: and they that worship him must worship him in spirit and in truth* (John 4.24). Hence we have some of the same spiritual characteristics as God.

Here are seven characteristics of God that we can reflect in life and ministry. The first principle is found in Genesis 1.1, *In the beginning God created the heaven and the earth.* The first thing that the mature believer seeks to do is to reflect the creative nature of God. God is the original creator, and is therefore infinitely creative. He has the ability and power to create or produce something, where there was nothing prior. God has the ability to affect entities with positive results. Simply put, God can and does make things happen because God is creative.

As I reflect over my life I see shadows of God's creative power within me. I notice that with God's help I can creative positivity. I can create relationships, meaningful events, and connections. I have been used of God to create an atmosphere of love, peace and joy. I have even brought about positive outcomes from negative situations. Has God been able to flow creatively through you in your life? Not just in sermons you preach, but also in your relationships, mentoring connections, and service to others. Use your reflective powers to examine you have been an agent of creativity to this fallen world.

I saw creativity and innovation reflected in my sister as she served others in our community. She took discarded purses and filled them with personal hygiene items and gave them to homeless women in need around the city of Detroit. How Godly creative was this idea? She took that which had been deemed worthless and useless, and used it for a positive purpose. This way of repurposing items and giving them new value is one of the ways we can reflect God's glory and creativity in our lives.

In what ways have you reflected God's creative nature in your life? What things have you affected for positive results? As a minister of God, how are you allowing your God-given creativity to reflect God's glory? Are you one of the countless people living life and not creating anything? It is our obligation to create good communities, churches, families and relationships! Be creative and CREATE something good. Only you have the power to create a life that is pleasing to God.

The second principle I learned is from Genesis 1.2, which states, *And the earth was without form, and void; and darkness was upon the face of the deep. And the Spirit of God moved upon the face of the waters.* I concentrated on the phrase, *the Spirit of God moved* and I began to understand that God is active in a chaotic world. God exercises motion, force and energy. In order to be like God, we must also remain active. Therefore it is a sin and not Godly at all, for anyone to be slothful.

Consider the following scriptures:

- Proverbs 15.19: *The way of the slothful man is as an hedge of thorns: but the way of the righteous is made plain.*

- Proverbs 21.25: *The desire of the slothful kills him; for his hands refuse to labor.*

- Hebrews 6.11: *And we desire that every one of you do show the same diligence to the full assurance of hope to the end: That ye be not slothful, but followers of them who through faith and patience inherit the promise.*

We cannot sit around and wait for others to do for us. True believers get up and do for themselves and others. They make things happen. God only rested on day seven, so we must also adhere to a 6:1 ratio of work to rest.

Let me be clear, being active does not mean that you have all the answers in life. Rather in all of your activity you are steadily pursuing God. Understand that it is perfectly ok, and in divine order, to change a plan as long as you are actively pursuing a plan. We must remain in forward motion, joyously seeking God's direction for our next step.

What are you doing for God? What are you giving God to work with?

I once met a fellow that was insistent that he would travel to a foreign field to minister the Gospel. He told me that he prayed earnestly for an opportunity to open up and until then he would just wait. I thought to myself, how foolish is this? Waiting on the Lord does not exempt us from activity. Yet, there was no intention to act or even to prepare to act in this man. He could have been preparing by presenting his life and message to those around him. He could have been proving his faithfulness with small things until bigger things opened up. God is not pleased when we sit on our God-given talents like this misguided man. Instead, we must put our gifts into action right where we are and then allow God to show us where He would have us to go next.

The third and fourth concepts I learned were recorded in Genesis 1.3-4 which states, *And God said, Let there be light: and there was light. And God saw the light, that it was good: and God divided the light from the darkness.* These next two points go together hand in hand. God said and God saw. God said to a formless mass of earth, "Let there be light." This has huge implications for us as believers. It tells us that God is willing to get involved in situations outside of Himself for the betterment of others, namely us. God has always been involved and will remain involved in our lives. He affects everything for the better.

Similarly, I take all that I am and seek to influence others around me in Godly ways. It is tempting to think that if you are not impacted by a particular problem, there is no need for you to be a part of the solution. This attitude is contrary to the nature of God. God sees and speaks. In other words God gets involved and influences His environment. We cannot reflect God in our life and ministry if we fail to get involved with and influence others.

The fifth point we can gauge from this passage of Scripture in Genesis is that God is observant. He sits high but looks low. God is observing the scenes on earth from heaven. Why does God watch over us? Because He is concerned about us. God does not peep into our lives like a bored housewife watching reality television, rather He watches over us because He loves us. As ministers, we must to be continuously observant as well. It is our responsibility to look at our surroundings, family, community, church, and world in search of opportunities to be creative, active, and involved.

The sixth thing I learned was recorded in Genesis 1.5, *And God called the light Day, and the darkness he called Night. And the evening and the morning were the first day.* Here God displays elements of his nature by taking responsibility, dominion and ownership. God's relationship to all of creation is that of responsibility. Ungodly people run from responsibility, but those that are reflecting glory and living a life of ministry rise to responsibility because it is in their nature.

In the text God takes on the responsibility of preparing the earth to fulfill its purpose in salvific history. Displayed all throughout the Bible, God takes responsibility for others. God is faithful to us and swears by his own Name, to have ownership of us. This responsibility is not fair-weather, for we see over and over again that God continues to claim us in good times and in bad.

Multiple scriptures reflect the ways that God takes responsibility for us as his children:

Leviticus 26.12, *And I will walk among you, and will be your God, and ye shall be my people.*

Genesis 12.2-3, *And I will make of you a great nation, and I will bless you, and make your name great; and you shalt be a blessing: And I will bless them that bless you, and curse him that curse you: and in you shall all families of the earth be blessed."*

Matthew records 18:6, *But whoever offends one of these little ones which believe in me, it would be better for him that a millstone were tied around his neck, and that he were drowned in the depth of the sea.*

Indeed we belong to the Lord and He is responsible for us. As ministers, it is therefore our reasonable service to look for ways that we can demonstrate our Godly nature by being responsible.

The concept that I gleaned from the text is best understood by looking at the passage as a whole.

In the beginning God created the heaven and the earth. And the earth was without form, and void; and darkness was upon the face of the deep. And the Spirit of God moved upon the face of the waters. And God said, Let there be light: and there was light. And God saw the light, that it was good: and God divided the light from the darkness. And God called the light Day, and the darkness he called Night. And the evening and the morning were the first day.

These words make it clear that God possesses intelligence. He knows how to create, move, see, say, and call. Put another way, God knows how to be creative, active, involved, observant, and responsible, and each of these characteristics flow out of his intelligence.

In this creation narrative it is clear that God was not only knowledgeable enough to know what to do, but He was also wise enough to know how to do. God possessed the foreknowledge to know that earth needed to be created and that it needed light. God used His knowledge and intellect to accomplish His will.

Each of us was created with the intellect, wisdom and knowledge needed to do good works. We should be wise enough to know our culture and environment and to get involved and when appropriate. You have access to a variety of Godly characteristics and you possess the wisdom to know when and how to apply them; will you be courageous enough to move forward in your ministry?

The final point I would like to demonstrate from the description of creation comes from Genesis 1.26, *And God said, Let us make man in our image, after our likeness.* It can be inferred from the text that God created us to be in relationship with together. If this is true, then relationship is in our nature. Throughout the Bible we see God engaging in relationships with His people. If God considers it important to interact with people, then we must also interact.

In my own life, I look for ways that I can learn to be more like God in every experience and every relationship. I look for ways to be creative, active, involved, observant, and responsible for my family, community and church. In fact, my entire ministry is built on tapping into my creativity to create beneficial relationships with my congregants, staff, students, and patients.

You need not wait a minute longer to walk in your ministry and life's purpose. Simply commit to getting involved and creatively solving a need that you have observed in your immediate community.

EPILOGUE

I remember many years ago I attended a church revival with a fiery young preacher. He excited the congregation with his astounding stories. One of the narratives that stuck with me was his story of running from God and ministry, and how God drew Him back into the fold. Once his car caught on fire, while he was inside of it, God had finally gotten the young man's attention. That day, he recommitted his life to Christ and made the decision to surrender to God's plan for his life.

I recall being depressed after hearing the preacher's rousing testimony, because I looked at my own life and did not see any experiences that were as exciting and miraculous. You see, I had not lived a riotous lifestyle. I hadn't slept with women through my college years, or abandoned the church or Biblical teachings. I simply did my best to live a life pleasing unto my God. I did enough sin to enter a sinner's hell and had damaged my relationship with God on several occasions but I tried my best. A few minutes into my sulking I realized that the seemingly unexciting life I had lived in my youth *is* my testimony. It was a testament that God can call you, set you apart, and keep you from a very young age.

While it is not my intention to discredit the young preacher's testimony, I do want to speak against the culture of sensationalism that has emerged in our church today. If we are not careful this appetite for the dramatic will restrict us to only seeing God in the BIG events, and cause us to miss the activity of God in our everyday lives.

I wrote this book to help you see that God is active in your life right now, and you don't have to be a televangelist to be great in God's eyes or to lead an effective ministry. Most of us will never pastor churches of twenty thousand or preach to millions, but God will use your life story and relationships, however simple or complex they might be, to bring Him Glory. Your journey is important to God. So enjoy your trip as God uses each experience to shape you into the person and minster you are to become. Continue to be MADE for ministry.

Blessed Journey,

Dr. Tony Shomari Marshall

APPENDIX

REFLECTION QUESTIONS FOR INDIVIDUALS AND GROUPS

Chapter 1: The Plan

1. How is God yet making you into who you are?

2. Can you see the hand of God pushing and pulling you to be better than you are?

3. How is God using your past learned behaviors and attitudes to bring about glory in your current situations?

4. What is ministry really?

Chapter 2: The Journey

1. Has God looked into the world and selected you to labor in a particular aspect of ministry?

2. Is this really what God desires for you to do?

3. Why am you pursuing public ministry?

4. What do you expect to gain from this?

5. What are you willing to give up for the sake of ministry?

6. Where is God leading you?

7. How are you gifted for ministry?

8. What type of ministry has God called you to?

9. Throughout your life, have you found yourself in places that were unpleasant, hostile and perhaps even dangerous?

10. What if God's desire for your ministry does not match your desire for your ministry?

Chapter 3: The Process

1. Has God ever made a connection in your life that you

perhaps did not see the benefit of until several years later?

2. Have you lived and matured enough to see how God works things out in your life?

3. So what is the process of maturity in faith?

4. How does God mature us into who we are to become?

5. Have you ever noticed that you tell your stories differently as time progresses? Why?

6. Have you ever experienced great pain and wondered how did God felt at that very moment?

Chapter 4: The Relationships

1. How have you, through your obedience, provided God the opportunity to birth a blessing in your life?

2. Have you been so busy praying against all hardship that you refuse to experience the gloom of the cross with Christ, thus limiting the glory of the resurrection?

3. Has the classroom of life taught you the importance of your personal relationship with Christ?

4. Have you ever suffered and it turned out to be for your good?

5. Can you see this principle in others and yourself?

6. Has God ever had to move you from your surroundings to reveal certain truths to you?

7. Do you know who you are to yourself?

8. Do you know who you are to God?

9. Have you come to know your strengths and limitations in God with regards to your personhood and ministry?

10. Have you grown to the place where you can see opportunity for growth in every situation?

11. Have you ever seen others too stubborn to learn, and thus doomed to never grow?

Chapter 5: The Classroom of life

1. Can you see how Diane's relationships and experiences hindered her ability to reflect and learn?

2. In what ways has your ability to learn and develop been hindered?

3. How can you actively remove those hindrances?

4. Have you carefully thought about how your cultural background influences your life and ministry?

5. Do you select friends that will foster a holy environment for your spiritual growth?

Chapter 6: The Lessons

1. Have you ever noticed that certain traits and lessons seemingly keep resurfacing in your life?

2. Have you ever wondered why people seem to make the same poor decisions over and over again

3. Are you mature enough to know that you need to learn?

4. Are there certain types of people that you have difficulty connecting with? If so, why?

5. Are they certain types of people that you love to connect with? If so, why?

6. What do you look to gain from your friendships?

7. Has fear compelled you to run away from certain situations?

Chapter 7: The Courage To Be

1. What does a successful life look like according to God's standards?

2. Has God been able to flow creatively through you in your life?

3. In what ways have you reflected God's creative nature in your life?

4. What things have you affected for positive results?

5. As a minister of God, how are you allowing your God-given creativity to reflect God's glory?

6. Are you one of the countless people living life and not creating anything?

7. What are you doing and going to do for God?

ABOUT THE AUTHOR

Tony Shomari Marshall is the eldest son of Tony and Judy Marshall. He was born and raised in Detroit, Michigan. He is the husband of Lady Chantell Marshall and the father of two daughters: Tiajah Shomara and Talaya Shomar.

Tony received a Bachelor of Arts degree in Biblical Literature and Biblical Languages from Taylor University. He received a Master of Divinity degree from Trinity Evangelical Divinity School in Deerfield, Illinois and completed his Doctor of Ministry degree at Andersonville Theological Seminary in Camille, Georgia. Tony also completed a Post-Graduate Fellowship at Ecumenical Theological Seminary in Detroit, Michigan. Dr. Marshall furthered his study of theology and human behavior at the Spiritual Care and Education Center of Toledo, Ohio. He is currently a Supervisory Candidate concentrating on Relational and Liberation Theology, Developmental Psychology, and Social Learning Theory as they interact with Human Spirituality within Pastoral Care.

Pastor Tony Marshall is the founding pastor of the House of Prayer Institutional Church of God in Christ. He served for 5 years as professor of Christian Thought and Philosophy at William Tyndale College. Currently he serves as the Director of Spiritual Support and Coordinator of Clinical Pastoral Education at Beaumont Health. Dr. Marshall is a board certified chaplain, a minister and member of several national ministry and chaplaincy associations including but not limited to the Association of Clinical Pastoral Education, Association of Professional Chaplains and the Southeastern Michigan Healthcare Chaplains Association.

Within the Church of God in Christ he is the Administrative Assistant to the Bishop Rance Lee Allen and functions as the Chief Operating Officer of the Michigan Northwestern Harvest Ecclesiastical Jurisdiction. He is a sought after speaker carrying on the tradition of Holiness to all facets of our post-modern generation.

NOTES

Quotations from the Bible in this work are from the King James Version, or are Tony Shomari Marshall's direct translations from the Hebrew and Greek text.

[i] *De captivitate Babylonica ecclesiae praeludium* [*Prelude concerning the Babylonian Captivity of the church*], *Weimar Ausgabe* 6, 564.6–14 as quoted in Norman Nagel, "Luther and the Priesthood of All Believers," Concordia Theological Quarterly 61 (October 1997) 4:283-84. Martin Luther writes, "How then if they are forced to admit that we are all equally priests, as many of us as are baptized, and by this way we truly are; while to them is committed only the Ministry (*ministerium Predigtamt*) and consented to by us (*nostro consensu*)? ... , for thus it says in 1 Peter 2, "You are a chosen race, a royal priesthood, a priestly kingdom." In this way we are all priests, as many of us as are Christians. There are indeed priests whom we call ministers. They are chosen from among us, and who do everything in our name. That is a priesthood which is nothing else than the Ministry. Thus 1 Corinthians 4:1: "No one should regard us as anything else than ministers of Christ and dispensers of the mysteries of God".

[ii] Nurture that is Christian, edited by James C. Wilhoit and John M. Dettoni, Baker Academic 1995

[iii] Term used in this way first by Erik Erikson in Identity Youth and Crisis, 1968 as a developmental psychology term used to describe psychological development as the result of an ongoing, bi-directional interchange between heredity and the environment. This view encompasses all of the possible developing factors on an organism and how they not only influence the organism and each other, but how the organism also influences its own development.

[iv] V. Bailey Gillespie "The Experience of Faith" Religious Education Press Birmingham Alabama, 1988 Gillespie writes, "Many recent theorist, seeing some repeating patterns in human development and growth, have postulated models to organize and explain the various

characteristics in those sequences of life. There have been basically four kinds of models postulated: 1). Developmental crisis models; 2). Structural growth models;. 3). Cognitive development stage models; and 4). Psychological growth models. p.67

[v] Henri Nouwen "In the Name of Jesus" Reflections of Christian Leadership Crossroads Publishing Company 1992

[vi] Thomas Jay Oord is a professor at <u>Northwest Nazarene University</u> in <u>Nampa, Idaho</u>. He is the author or editor of nearly twenty books on Relational Theology, <u>Open Theism</u>, <u>P</u>ostmodernity, <u>Wesleyan</u> Thought, <u>Holiness</u>, and <u>Evangelical</u> Theology.

[vii] James Cone teaches that suffering is a reality for the Christian living in this present age. He also knows that through experiences of suffering, God is at work to produce endurance and ultimately maturity. For this reason, the child of God should respond not with fear or frustration but rather with pure joy.

[viii] Thomas Jay Oord "What is Relational Theology" Relational Theology: A contemporary Introduction *Wipf* and Stock Publishing, San Diego 2012

"The Bible describes the activities and nature of a relational God…God's interaction with Adam and Eve portray God as relational" p.1

[ix] Thomas Jay Oord, "Relational Holiness: Responding to the Call of Love" Beacon Hill Kansas City 2005. According to the relational holiness proposal, God is the most important actor in everyone's environment. God affects all others and does so in every moment.

[x] James Cone's God of the Oppressed, "Divine Liberation and Black Suffering,"

"Whatever else may be said about the philosophical difficulties that the problem of evil poses whether in the traditional definition of classical philosophy or in Albert Camus's humanism or even in the black humanism of William Jones and Anthony Pinn, faith arising out of the cross and resurrection of Jesus renders their questions (Is God evil? or Is God a white racist?) absurd from the biblical point of view. The absurdity of the question is derived from the fact that its origin ignores the very foundation of biblical faith itself, that is, <u>God becoming the Suffering Servant in Christ in order that we might be</u>

liberated from injustice and pain."-page 162

[xi] James Cone, *A Black Theology of Liberation, 40th Anniversary ed.* (Maryknoll: Orbis Books, 2010), *xxiii*.

[xii] Oord argues in Relational Holiness for mutuality not equality in our relationship with God. He holds God is open to and affected by us, because both the Creator and the creatures enjoy mutual relations. To say that these relations are mutual is to say that God interacts with us and we interact with God. It is not to say that God and creatures are equal. The wonder of it all is that the God of the universe enjoys give-and-receive relations with everything that exists. Envisioning God and creatures as relational beings resides at the heart of relational holiness.

[xiii] This was a teaching that I received from Dr. Martin Luther King Jr. He believed and taught that every person's worth lies in their relatedness to God. King taught that an individual has value because God confers it on her. He taught in Stride Toward Freedom: The Montgomery Story. Harper and Brothers 1984, that those most agonizing, dehumanizing, and unbearable moments of his life were the very same moments that he felt closest to God.

[xiv] Martin Luther King Jr. wrote in *Where do we Go from Here*, "The image of God is universally shared in equal portions by all men . . . . Every human being has etched in his personality the indelible stamp of the Creator. Every man must be respected because God loves him. The worth of an individual does not lie in the measure of his intellect, his racial origin, or his social position. Human worth lies in relatedness to God. An individual has value because he has value to God. Whenever this is recognized, "whiteness" and blackness" pass away as determinants in a relationship and "son" and "brother" are substituted.

[xv] The term double consciousness was first presented by W. E. B. Dubois. It refers to African Americans struggle with a multi-faceted conception of self; when one is constantly trying to reconcile the two cultures that compose one's single identity.

[xvi] I pride myself in being open to all people. I believe that learning is enhanced when we interact with those that are different. Thus I have offered CPE to many different and diverse people. Hindu, Muslim,

Judaism, Catholicism and many different protestant denominations, LGBT, African American, Latino Americans, European American, Native Americans and Africans just to name a few, have all been people of mine over my years of training.

[xvii] David Augsburger. Pastoral Counseling Across Cultures. The Westminster Press. Philadelphia, Pennsylvania. 1986

[xviii] Bandura, Albert. Social Learning Theory. New Jersey: Prentice Hall 1977 Bandura wrote, "Most human behavior is learned observationally through modeling: from observing others, one forms an idea of how new behaviors are performed, and on later occasions this coded information serves as a guide for action".

[xix] Kolb, D.A. Experiential Learning: Experience as the source of learning and development. Englewood Cliffs, NJ: Prentice Hall 1984 p.41. Kolb expresses that an experiential learning theory "offers a fundamentally different view of the learning process from that of the behavioral theories of learning based on an empirical epistemology or the more implicit theories of learning which underlie traditional educational methods, methods that are for the most part based on a rational, idealist epistemology."

[xx] According to Kolb learning and experience are connected and ever changing he writes, "No two thoughts are ever the same, since experience always intervenes" p.26

[xxi] David Kolb Learning Theory Cycle

[xxii] The concept of "Jesus as a CPE supervisor" or at least a model of teaching that was reflective of Christ Biblical model of teaching was first introduced to me in Kenneth Pohly's work transforming the Rough Places. He presents several thoughts from Ron Sutherland regarding Jesus teaching model such as: inviting people to share, small groups, intimacy, relationship, entrusting his disciples and several others. p. 99

[xxiii] Palmer, Parker J. The Courage to Teach. San Francisco: Jossey-Bass Publishers, 1998.

[xxiv] I adhere to the power of story-telling as presented by Michael White and Daivid Epston in *Narrative Means to Therapeutic Ends*. W.W. Norton and Company New York 1990. They understand that in the retelling of personal stories people shape the retelling according to

where they are emotionally. This become very helpful in discovering how people have grown from previous events in life.

[xxv] Gerald Corey Brooks. Theory and Practice of Group Counseling. Cole Publishing Belmont CA 1990 p.490 Gerald Corey writes of personal centered group therapy, "Our job is to facilitate not direct, this group. In part, this means helping to make it an accepting and caring group".

[xxvi] According to Bandura, when human development is viewed from a lifespan perspective, the influential determinants include a varied succession of life events that vary in their power to affect the direction lives take. Many of these determinants include age-graded social influences that are provided by custom within familial, educational, and other institutional systems. Some involve biological conditions that exercise influence over person's futures. Others are unpredictable occurrences in the physical environment. Still others involve irregular life events such as career changes, divorce, migration, accidents, and illness.

[xxvii] Jawanza Kunjufu is an educator and social critic. He earned his Ph.D. from Union Graduate School. He has authored 33 books examining the effects of culture on black boys including national best sellers, Black People: Middle Class Teachers; Keeping Black Boys out of Special Education; An African Centered Response to Ruby Payne's Poverty Theory; Raising Black Boys; 200 Plus Educational Strategies to Teach Children of Color; and his latest title, Understanding Black Male Learning Styles.

[xxviii] Arthur Warmoth, Culture, Somas, and Human Development, *Somatics* Magazine-Journal, vol. XIII (no. 1), Fall-Winter 2000-01 Arthur Warmoth writes, "it is culture that is the fundamental enabler and expression of distinctly human life".

[xxix] In Identity Youth and Crisis Erikson writes, "each successive step, then, is a potential crisis because of a radical change in perspective. Crisis is used … in a developmental sense to connote not a threat or catastrophe, but a turning point, a crucial period of increased vulnerability and heightened potential, and therefore, the ontogenetic source of generational strength and maladjustment". W.W. Norton and Company new York 1968 p. 96

xxx Erik Erikson. Identity and the Life Cycle. W. W. Norton and Company New York 1980. In Identity and the Life Cycle, Erikson purposes a theory of psychosocial development consisting of eight stages of which a healthy developing human shall encounter from infancy through adulthood. In each stage the person encounters crises and optimistically passes until a new crisis moment is encountered. Each stages is epigenetic in that is builds upon the previous experience. The stages are: trust vs. mistrust, autonomy vs. shame, initiative vs. guilt, industry vs. inferiority, identity vs. role confusion, intimacy vs. isolation, generativity vs. stagnation.

xxxi Epigentic according to Erikson is the idea that human development is governed by a sequence of stages that depend on genetic or hereditary substance

xxxii James Wilhiot and John Dettoni. Nurture that is Christian: Developmental Perspectives on Christian Education Baker, Grand Rapids 1995

xxxiii Judith Jordan. Relational-Cultural Therapy, Theories of Psychotherapy Series. Eds. Jon Carlson and matt Englar-Carlson (Washington, D.C.: American Psychological Association 2010)

xxxiv A goal of RCT is to create and maintain Mutually-Growth-Fostering Relationships, in which both parties feel that they are important and matter. In MGFRs, all those involved experience; 1) a desire to move into more relationships; 2) energy or excitement regarding relationships; 3) increased knowledge of oneself and the other person in the relationship; 4) a desire to take action both in the growth-fostering relationship and outside of it; 5) an overall increased sense of worth.[3]

xxxv This truth is evidently supported from my analysis of our group discussion of the Ferguson case referenced in my Education paper.

xxxvi Jordan p. 49

xxxvii Michael White, & David Epston. *Narrative means to therapeutic ends.* New York: WW Norton 1990. Narrative therapy involves a process of making meaning through the retelling of story. The narrative therapist works with the client in the process of developing richer narratives. Questions are asked to generate experientially vivid descriptions of life events that are not currently included in the plot of the problematic story.

[xxxviii] Gerald Corey Theory and Practice of Group Counseling Gerald Corey Brooks /Cole Publishing Belmont CA 1990

Made in United States
North Haven, CT
24 January 2024

47851913R00071